Race, Diversity, and Social Mobility in the Public Relations Industry

This book explores the recent academic and practice-based research and thinking on race, diversity, and social mobility within the public relations industry, arguing for the necessity of more transformative actions to address systemic inequities.

Through an analysis of interviews with UK-based public relations practitioners from a wide range of backgrounds, this book integrates and illustrates different strands of research to shed light on persistent challenges and opportunities in the field and understand how those who are often the subjects of such discussions experience discrimination. The authors introduce complex topics in an accessible manner, providing an overview of recent research, demonstrating practical applications of theoretical frameworks, and suggesting reading for further exploration. It also includes additional pedagogical features which allow readers to explore specific topics through guided reading and exploratory questions.

By grounding its analysis in the lived experiences of public relations practitioners, this book contributes to the literature of race, diversity, and social mobility while fostering discussion on the systematic discrimination faced by practitioners. It will help and encourage researchers, educators, and practitioners to critically explore their own practice and open up new conversations about this crucial issue.

Elizabeth Bridgen is Head of Academic Development (Partner Provision) at Buckinghamshire New University, UK. She was formerly Principal Lecturer in Public Relations at Sheffield Hallam University, UK. Her research mainly explores the lived experience of public practitioners with a focus on those who are often excluded from mainstream scholarship. She is co-editor with Sarah Williams of *Women's Work in Public Relations* (2024), to which she also contributed a chapter "Just like any other: Public Relations Careers in the Adult Industries." She is also co-editor with Dejan Verčič of *Experiencing Public Relations: International Voices* and recently contributed chapters to the books *Towards a New Understanding of Masculine Habitus: Women in*

Leadership in Public Relations (Topic, 2023), *Gender and Freelancing in the Communication Industries: Experiences, Practices, Discourses* (Anton and Moise, 2025).

She has published in academic journals including *Journal of Communication Management, PRism,* and *Journal of Media Practice and Education*, and *Effects of Education Learning in Digital Learning Environments* (Duarte, Andrade, and Dias, 2025).

Ileana Zeler, PhD, is Associate Professor in the Department of Advertising, Public Relations, and Audiovisual Communication at the Universitat Autònoma de Barcelona, Spain. She earned her PhD in Communication at the Universitat Rovira i Virgili, where her dissertation received international distinction and honours. Her research focuses on public relations and strategic communication, with a particular interest in communication management in digital contexts, gender challenges within the industry, and sustainability. Her work is featured in high-impact journals, including the *Journal of Communication Management*, *Corporate Communications: An International Journal*, and the *International Journal of Strategic Communication.*

In addition to her research, Ileana is a guest professor at universities across Spain, Latin America, and Europe. She currently serves as Chair of the Organisational and Strategic Communication Section of the European Communication Research and Education Association (ECREA). She is an active member of associations such as Euprera and AIRP and co-founder of AcadémicasPR, a network dedicated to fostering research about and for women academics in public relations, advocating for structural changes in academia and the professional field.

Global PR Insights

This innovative series of short-form books provides a new forum to critically evaluate contemporary scholarship and global practice in all aspects of PR and communications. It aims to promote and provoke new ways of thinking, providing an opportunity to reframe public relations beyond traditional frameworks, reflecting new interpretations, emerging research, and insights from different fields. One goal of the series is to bridge the perceived gap between the "academics" and "professionals" in the PR and communications fields, and to introduce diverse voices discussing theories and practice in the global economy. The concise format (20-40,000 words) offers both new and established scholars an accessible and supportive opportunity for publishing and disseminating new ideas and emerging research.

About the Series Editor: Donnalyn Pompper is Professor, Endowed Chair in Public Relations at the University of Oregon, USA. She is the author of several books, has published extensively in peer-reviewed academic journals and also has 25 years of practical experience as a public relations manager and journalist prior to joining the academy.

Strategic Communication and AI
Public Relations with Intelligent User Interfaces
Simon Moore and Roland Hübscher

Artificial Intelligence, Strategic Communicators and Activism
Lukasz Swiatek, Marina Vujnovic, Chris Galloway and Dean Kruckeberg

Cultural Transformations
Nigerian Women Leading Public Relations
Ana Adi and Tolulope Olorundero

Race, Diversity, and Social Mobility in the Public Relations Industry
Elizabeth Bridgen and Ileana Zeler

For more information about this series, please visit: https://www.routledge.com/Global-PR-Insights/book-series/GPRI

Race, Diversity, and Social Mobility in the Public Relations Industry

Elizabeth Bridgen and Ileana Zeler

Routledge
Taylor & Francis Group
LONDON AND NEW YORK

First published 2025
by Routledge
4 Park Square, Milton Park, Abingdon, Oxon OX14 4RN

and by Routledge
605 Third Avenue, New York, NY 10158

Routledge is an imprint of the Taylor & Francis Group, an informa business

British Library Cataloguing-in-Publication Data
A catalogue record for this book is available from the British Library

ISBN: 978-1-032-69211-1 (hbk)
ISBN: 978-1-032-69219-7 (pbk)
ISBN: 978-1-032-69223-4 (ebk)

DOI: 10.4324/9781032692234

Typeset in Times New Roman
by codeMantra

The authors are profoundly thankful to the public relations practitioners interviewed who generously shared their time and valuable insights and to the administrators of the training programmes who facilitated our access to their students and graduates.

Contents

Pedagogical features

Introduction and Rationale

The origins of this book can be traced back to 2017/2018 when one of the authors embarked on a research project to explore the impact of initiatives—usually called "programmes" in the United Kingdom (UK) but referred to as "schemes" in some texts—designed to increase diversity within the professional realm of public relations. This research was qualitative in design and was conducted through interviews with graduates of the Taylor Bennett Foundation, a British initiative designed to enhance Black, Asian, and ethnic minority representation within the public relations industry. Some of those findings were presented in a Chartered Institute of Public Relations book (2018) which was published to celebrate the organisation's 70th anniversary. The longer-term intention was to develop the research for publication in an academic journal.

However, the evolution of this project encountered various obstacles, including the constraints of professional and academic obligations, health setbacks experienced by one of the authors, and the disruptive impact of the Covid-19 pandemic. Yet, it was not just these practical challenges that reshaped the trajectory of the endeavour. The brutal 2020 murder of George Perry Floyd Jr., a Black American man who was murdered by a white police officer in Minneapolis, Minnesota during an arrest, ignited a global reckoning on systemic racism and social justice. This watershed moment catalysed a profound shift in societal consciousness, compelling a critical examination of prevailing norms and practices within professional spheres.

The growth of the Black Lives Matter movement and the attention it received in the wider public sphere further amplified voices that had long been marginalised, prompting a re-evaluation of entrenched beliefs and attitudes. What became increasingly apparent was a transformation in the discourse surrounding diversity and inclusion within the public relations profession. That meant that some of the views suggested by the interviewees—and the phrasing of the questions—began to sound slightly dated against the backdrop of a rapidly evolving landscape. The narrative had shifted. We had moved from an occupational space where, in the 2017 interviews, some Black, Asian, and ethnic minority practitioners interviewed claimed that colour did not matter to a place where race assumed a central role in discussions concerning

DOI: 10.4324/9781032692234-1

recruitment, retention and the cultivation of diversity within the workplace. While the interviews represented a moment in time, the discourse in the public relations profession had developed—even if corporate action has not, as the book explains.

In 2023, the opportunity to write this book allowed the authors the time and opportunity to revisit the initial interviews and expand the data collection efforts. While race remains at the centre of the book, the exploration is alongside (and in combination with) other factors which affect social mobility in the public relations industry. These factors encompass, but are not limited to, religion, ethnicity, social class, accent, geographical location, gender, sexuality, disability, neurodiversity, and age. By incorporating a diverse array of perspectives on these and other dimensions of diversity, equality, and inclusion in the workplace, we endeavour to offer a short but comprehensive examination of the multifaceted landscape of public relations and communications.

This book explores the recent advancements in theoretical frameworks and empirical research pertaining to race, diversity, and social mobility in the public relations industry. It also advocates for the necessity of radical action to address entrenched disparities and foster a more inclusive professional environment.

The foundation of the social justice case for diversity, equality, and inclusion rests upon the principle that every individual should have equal access to employment opportunities, training, and development based solely on merit and that everyone should have the right to be free of any direct or indirect discrimination and harassment or bullying. While this appears straightforward, research shows (e.g., Chartered Institute of Public Relations, 2020, 2022b, 2024; Social Mobility Commission, 2022) that the reality often diverges from this ideal, as we shall uncover in the subsequent chapters.

Starting with a review of both academic and practice-based literature and reports, this book draws together different strands of research through the analysis of interviews with public relations practitioners from diverse backgrounds, some of whom have graduated from training programmes designed to either increase the number of people from minority groups into the British public relations industry or raise the number of public relations leaders from diverse backgrounds. Such initiatives operate by giving Black, Asian, and ethnic minority and other practitioners from disadvantaged groups the skills, knowledge, and contacts to succeed in an area, which is dominated by white, middle-class and privately educated practitioners (Chartered Institute of Public Relations, 2022a,b) and which according to Gregory (2022, p. 401) "does not open its doors, make welcome, reward or honour its own diverse community." However, we also interviewed practitioners who had forged careers in public relations in other ways.

Where practitioners had been graduates of training programmes, these interviews collected stories from graduates of from the Taylor Bennett Foundation training public relations programme, a short, UK-based intensive course run in partnership with leading public relations agencies designed to help Black, Asian, and ethnic minority graduates move into public relations, and from Socially Mobile, which delivers training to those from lower socio-economic backgrounds as well as under-represented and under-served groups including Black, Asian, and ethnic minority practitioners, the LGBTQ+ community, women returners, and those with disability.

Grounded in critical race theory and informed by seminal works in the field of diversity and public relations such as Edwards (2014a), Logan (2023) and Pompper (2005, 2013), this book elucidates key themes derived from the interviews:

- Whether leadership and social mobility programmes help to increase awareness of diversity issues and how they help the practitioners they are designed to support;
- The benefits of a diverse public relations workforce and the issues with the "business case for diversity";
- Recruitment and retention of a diverse workforce;
- Whether programmes to aid diversity, while making a difference to the lives of some practitioners, are also reproducing hegemony/white privilege;
- How factors such as race, class, and geographical location intersect and the difference that this intersectionality makes to career success and stability in the occupation of public relations;
- How and where Black, Asian, and ethnic minority practitioners and those from other diverse backgrounds experience and view discrimination in the public relations industry.

Recent industry research has shown that while there are plenty of initiatives, reports, training, and resources designed to increase representation of people from minority backgrounds in public relations, one of the main issues is retention. Nevertheless, the CIPR's Race and Public Relations report (2020) suggested that, despite all the effort given by thought leaders and professional associations to making the occupation more diverse, ethnic diversity within the public relations industry had apparently declined from 11% in 2015 to 8% in 2019 despite considerable industry initiatives to address this challenge. This decline was also noted in the NHS Communications report (2024).

The Chair of CIPR's Diversity and Inclusion Forum, Avril Lee, said at the time:

> The PR industry agrees that diversity is important for attracting the best talent to bring fresh thinking, creativity and insights into new audiences, but our actions speak louder than our words. And our actions are building a profession of white private-school alumni; we are less diverse than we've been for the past five years.
>
> (Chartered Institute of Public Relations, 2020, p. 9)

The CIPR's report highlighted not only recruitment challenges but also retention issues, which together not only contribute to poor diversity metrics but starkly highlight the issues the sector faces if it is to truly represent the population it serves. Interviews carried out by the Chartered Institute of Public Relations report authors underscored the lack of attention given to retention in diversity discussions within the profession. Neglecting retention could inadvertently lead individuals into a profession where discrimination persists, and where efforts to increase representation are insufficient (Chartered Institute of Public Relations, 2020, p. 10). Consistent themes emerged from both the report's findings and our interviewees in Chapter 2, including instances of racism, an inflexible and non-inclusive culture, limited equal opportunities for advancement, and unconscious bias from colleagues and clients.

There is plenty to unpick from the CIPR's report and alongside this we observe a growing body of literature and media content exploring race, diversity, social mobility and public relations ranging from academic articles to YouTube videos, from LinkedIn posts to industry reports. However, we recognise the complexity of this area for practitioners and academics, and one where many are nervous of "saying the wrong thing" or not being sure what they can do.

The short format of this book enables an introduction of complex topics relating to race, diversity, and social mobility in a manner accessible to both practitioners and scholars. Leveraging the aggregate and individual voices of those we have interviewed, we strive to breathe life into intricate ideas. By linking the critical research to interview narratives, the book puts concepts and ideas into everyday language and encourages readers to look at the meaning of what is said and the multiple struggles faced by practitioners.

Furthermore, this book serves as a resource for academics, offering an overview of recent research and guiding further reading. There are also pedagogical features such as extended interview extracts where the reader can explore issues in more depth, guided by some thoughtful questions. It also demonstrates the practical application of theory to real-world situations, highlighting the value of academic research in addressing contemporary challenges within the public relations profession.

1 Foundations of Change

Understanding Race, Diversity and Social Mobility in the Public Relations Industry

Introduction

This chapter's starting point is to explore recent literature on critical race theory and its intersection with public relations, linking it to discussions on diversity and social mobility. Our aim is to provide a theoretical foundation for understanding the complex dynamics at play in the landscape of public relations practice.

Drawing on Edwards (2014a) work, this book explores diversity in public relations through three critical questions: (1) How does marginalisation shape experience?; (2) How does marginalisation shape life and identities?; and (3) How do ethnic minority practitioners respond to marginalisation as they pursue their careers? In her 2014 book, Edwards observed that race should be the analytical starting point for discussions about diversity in public relations—not just since it has been "neglected in their field of public relations and communication studies" (p. 12), but that putting it at the centre of the narrative demonstrates that race cannot be seen as just another aspect of identity. She acknowledged the complexity and intersectionality of the term "diversity" but used race as her "point of departure" to demonstrate how race and racism are "patterns of meaning that reflect the centrality of race to disadvantage or marginalisation" (Edwards, 2014a, p. 22).

This can be seen, for example, in public relations recruitment processes or in the area of staff retention where norms of whiteness and of particular behaviours are held to be a standard. This perspective is increasingly relevant as professional and academic literature is starting to recognise the multifaceted nature of discrimination and disadvantages both in the public relations industry and across other industry sectors affecting recruitment, career advancement, and employee retention. This book adopts Edwards' framework as a starting point, mindful that the recent industry focus on social mobility might potentially diminish attention to race and ethnicity as critical areas of study.

A recent conversation on LinkedIn between public relations professionals (PR Academy Ltd, 2024) highlighted the way that race intersects with other factors such as social class and gender to create multiple disadvantages. In this conversation, one professional argued that to consider social class as

DOI: 10.4324/9781032692234-2

a separate factor diminished the struggle faced by Black, Asian, and ethnic minority practitioners. This debate highlights the necessity for race to occupy a central position in research into the multiple factors affecting recruitment, progression, and job satisfaction in public relations. Vardeman-Winter and Place (2017) noted the need for researchers to "seriously engage in intersectional research that links diverse practitioners' experiences" (p. 326), with negative outcomes. These outcomes include salary discrepancies and a lack of opportunity for practitioners from marginalised backgrounds.

Scholarship on race and social mobility within the field of public relations is a growing area of interest, attracting attention from both academics and professionals, and has developed significantly over the last decade. Social movements around the world, such as Black Lives Matter, have brought issues of race and social injustice to the forefront, increasing mainstream awareness of the marginalised position of Black, Asian, and ethnic minority practitioners and the disadvantages they face in the workplace. In addition, social media empowers activist groups and allows individuals from diverse and under-represented backgrounds to find allies and share information, although not always equally with majority groups. This dynamic can both help and hinder moves to greater diversity as we shall explore later in the book.

While the intersection of race, class and place and its link to social mobility and oppression is the object of social scientific research (e.g., Anthias, 2013; Bilge, 2010; Moore-Berg & Karpinski, 2021), there has been little academic work in this area focusing specifically on public relations, although there are exceptions (e.g., Edwards, 2014a, 2023; Pompper, 2005, 2013; Vardeman-Winter et al., 2013).

It is worth noting before we address different aspects of diversity—if they ever can be considered in isolation—what we mean when we discuss the intersection of myriad disadvantages or diversities. As Anthias (2013, p. 125) observed:

> There cannot be a singular definition of an intersectionality framework as there is a great deal of diversity in the way it is theorized and applied […] its primary roots [are] within anti-racist feminism in the United States, being originally concerned with the particular forms of oppression faced by racialized women […]. However, the coinage of the term intersectionality has been attributed to Crenshaw (1994). It has been described as a 'fast travelling concept' (Knapp, 2005), and there are issues about transplanting the term to a range of other contexts.

Continuing this theme, Edwards (2023) summarised that "intersectionality is a central tenet of feminist scholarship that explores contextual dynamics of power in a wide range of fields, grounded in the need to address structural disadvantages not captured by analyses focussing only on one dimension of inequality" (p. 28). Edwards (2013) and Carbado (2013) argued that whiteness, maleness, and middle-class standards are normalised in public relations practice and therefore invisible. What this means in reality is that Black practitioners and those who do not belong to the norm always have to try to "fit" in with this dominant paradigm or in some cases exploit their difference for financial gain, career progression or social capital. While certain aspects, such as accent, social class, and sexual orientation, can often be masked—albeit with difficulty—others, like race, are immutable.

Beginning with Edwards' starting point of the centrality of race, we will first discuss race and critical race theory before moving on to explore different aspects of diversity.

Critical Race Theory and Public Relations

Critical race theory (CRT) scholars and activists seek to highlight and transform the relationships between and around race, racism, and power by situating them within broader perspectives that includes economics, history, setting, group and self-interest, emotions, and the unconscious (e.g., Delgado et al., 2023). CRT places race at the centre of inquiry, using it as the primary lens through which analyses of societal structures, systems, and institutions are developed (Logan, 2023). This focus not only highlights the significance of race but also proves particularly effective in uncovering hidden discrimination in specific contexts, including in the workplace and social interactions. Furthermore, CRT explores the intersections of personal forces such as disability, colour, gender, and sexuality and in wider areas of government and society such as immigration and globalisation. Scholars in the field argued that neutrality and objectivity are impossible; as Pompper (2005) observed: "writers such as Delgado (1989) argued that Whites fail to see how laws and rights affecting voting, homesteading, property inheritance, and jobs have positively shaped their realities; they see truth, when they should see their perspective" (p. 144).

Within the context of public relations, there are multiple forms of disadvantage which can be critically examined through the lens of CRT. In the United Kingdom (UK) and beyond, public relations has a gendered and racialised subculture that disadvantages both women and practitioners of colour (Edwards, 2023). This can be seen in a myriad of ways, including the marginalisation of individuals based on social class and ability/disability. In the public relations workplace, social capital is often valued in terms of, for instance, modes of dress, patterns of speech, and familiarity with corporate life and British political systems. These behaviours and practices are seen as the norm, rendering middle-class whiteness invisible and unremarkable, as it dominates the professional landscape of public relations. Data from the Chartered Institute of Public Relations (2022a, 2022b, 2024), demonstrated how those who deviate from this norm face disadvantages in terms of salary and career progression.

As Edwards (2023) observed, "[p]ractitioners of colour also face exclusionary practices including racial stereotyping, pigeonholing, discriminatory recruitment and promotion practices, racialized embodiment, and normative associations of whiteness with professionalism and leadership" (p. 31). However, Edwards also noted that race, along with other forms of difference, can be commodified and called upon when convenient—such as in instances where a public relations campaign requires particular cultural expertise. This phenomenon was frequently discussed in the interviews conducted in Chapter 2, where various participants expressed pride in helping their organisations connect with a particular stakeholder group or avoid cultural insensitivity. Yet this raises the question: Is their presence being commodified? Fraga et al. (2005) described this capitalisation on multiple identities as "strategic intersectionality," where attributes are reframed as advantageous rather than detrimental by both the individual and their employer or clients (Bridgen, 2018).

Ultimately, CRT offers valuable theoretical frameworks that empower us to combat racism and adopt an activist stance centred on recognising the inherent humanity of all individuals. This commitment extends both within organisations and beyond, as we strive to foster a more equitable society through public relations research and practice. As Waymer and Heath (2016) as well as Logan (2023) highlighted, it is also essential for critical scholars to actively engage in addressing racial injustice. They must embody the principles of CRT not only in their academic work but also through concrete actions that challenge systemic inequities.

Defining Diversity in the Context of Public Relations

The term "diversity" is highly subjective, never static, and can be used to both understand power relations in organisations and society, and to recognise individual experiences. Sha and Ford (2007) described diversity as encompassing both immutable characteristics, such as age and race, and mutable ones, like language and religion. Further, Childers Hon and Brunner (2000) expanded on this by framing diversity as a spectrum of complex issues related to gender, race, and other forms of discrimination, along with the social and legal responsibilities that businesses have to proactively manage these issues.

A deeper perspective, offered by Mayorga-Gallo (2019), suggests that diversity should be understood as an ideology rather than merely a discourse. This perspective emphasises the need to examine how the ideology of diversity is reflected in practices, policies, and justifications at various levels, from the individual to the institutional. Such an approach reveals how diversity is not just a concept to be discussed but an ideology that shapes and is shaped by organisational norms and societal structures.

Moreover, the definition and implications of diversity are influenced by the cultural context. Mor Barak (2000) highlighted that the understanding of diversity is deeply embedded in the cultural, social, and historical contexts of both the organisation and its society. Consequently, while diversity can be a common goal, its interpretation and implementation can vary significantly based on local cultural norms, societal values, and institutional practices. In this regard, Jackson and Joshi (2004) argued that a comprehensive understanding of diversity dynamics necessitates consideration of the social context as individual attitudes and behaviours alone cannot fully explain team dynamics. In support of this, Jones et al. (2020) highlighted that integrating diverse voices and perspectives within teams can lead to enhanced creativity and adaptability. This reinforces the notion that diversity is not merely about representation; rather, it is also about leveraging differences to achieve organisational goals.

In the public relations industry, diversity holds particular significance due to the field's role in shaping and reflecting societal narratives. However, the industry has often faced criticism for its lack of diversity, being predominantly dominated by a narrow demographic—mainly white and female practitioners—especially in a western context (Logan, 2011; Vardeman-Winter & Place, 2017). This limitation affects the field's effectiveness and relevance in an increasingly diverse world. Pompper (2005, p. 140) framed diversity within the public relations industry as a consideration of differences in race, ethnicity, and culture, which are essential for developing truly representative communication strategies. By embracing diversity, public relations can better serve its role as a bridge between organisations and the communities they engage with, fostering more inclusive and authentic dialogues that resonate across different cultural and social landscapes. Nevertheless, this is not seen often in practice. In a report on the UK's National Health Service—which serves all the UK's highly diverse population, it was noted that:

> [W]e are going backwards [in terms of ethnic diversity], with less than 5% of the most senior NHS communications professionals from an ethnic minority background. In addition, almost two thirds (61%) of senior NHS communicators say they do not have a communications workforce that is representative of the local communities they serve.
>
> (NHS Communicate, 2024, p. 5)

Research on diversity in public relations has been primarily focused on the U.S. (e.g., Logan, 2011; Pompper, 2013; Vardeman-Winter et al., 2013; Vardeman-Winter & Place, 2017). Nevertheless, significant contributions have also emerged from other regions, such as the UK (e.g., Edwards, 2014b) and Australia (e.g., Fitch & Third, 2010; Sison, 2016). Furthermore, a growing body of research is originating from elsewhere in the world, which this book attempts to explore and highlight (e.g. Abdullah, 2007; Al-Jenaibi, 2011).

Edwards and Aulakh (2024) recently outlined the main lines of research in this area, noting that many studies have focused on strategies to improve representation and integration within organisations, emphasising the crucial role of leadership in effectively advancing diversity efforts in the workplace. Similarly, scholars such as Austin et al. (2019), Ciszek and Logan (2018), and Vardeman and Sebesta (2020) explored how inequalities are perpetuated through communication practices, recognising that communication about inequality is complex and can sometimes lack the necessary impact, making authenticity essential. Vardeman-Winter and Place (2017) studied this issue from a societal perspective, observing "if there is a monochromatic/uniform cluster of identities represented among these organizations, the discourses will be limited to similar worldviews" (p. 328), and thus any effort to promote or explore diversity will be hampered by this setting. Additionally, recent studies (e.g., Ashby-King & Anderson, 2023; Men et al., 2023) have examined the role of public relations in conveying diversity, equity, and inclusion (DEI) policies and practices. While public relations has the potential to foster positive change, a recurring challenge is the gap between promises made and actions taken. This disconnect can create a "diversity paradox," where positive DEI messaging fails to translate into tangible actions, inadvertently sustaining existing inequalities.

Despite much rhetoric in the public relations industry, the regular bellwether Chartered Institute of Public Relations (2024) report, *State of the Profession*, did not consider equality and diversity as a "top five industry challenge" until 2024 when it was placed in fifth position, despite a previously acknowledged industry skills shortage and the need to understand the communication needs of a diverse global, regional, and local stakeholders (Chartered Institute of Public Relations, 2024). In the view of, for instance, Botan and Sommerfeldt (2023), public relations should be a multicultural endeavour that welcomes and makes room for more minority and female scholars, researchers, and practitioners.

Furthermore, the CIPR's 2020 report, *Race and Public Relations,* revealed stark findings, noting that a significant issue was the retention of diverse talent. The report cautioned that "[w]ithout addressing it, and focusing solely on recruitment, we risk encouraging those to enter a profession that may ultimately discriminate against them" (Chartered Institute of Public Relations, 2020, p. 9). In addition to retention issues, the report identified other critical barriers, including the lack of a "social circle" experienced by practitioners of colour due to parental background, discussed in the context of social class. Moreover, the cultural rigidity of many agencies forced many individuals to adopt "whiteness" to succeed, rather than encouraging workplaces to adapt and reflect the diversity of the society they serve.

Quite simply, despite multiple efforts across the industry to recruit diverse talent, retention remains a problem due to a range of complex and overlapping reasons. The CIPR's 2020 report highlighted the inflexible and non-inclusive culture of many workplaces, noting that there was a pressure to conform to the white "norm." This observation aligns with Edwards' (2014a, 2023) aforementioned discussion on the pervasive influence of "whiteness" in public relations, where she argues that the industry's Western-centric practices and norms persistently marginalise practitioners of colour. This emphasis on conformity extends to the value placed on "soft skills" and "chemistry" in professional interactions, as noted by Bourne (2022). These competencies, crucial for relationship-building in public relations, often operate in opaque ways, protecting the privileged access of white professionals to sought-after roles through informal hiring practices that are largely invisible and unquantified. Edwards (2014a) further concluded that without genuine acknowledgement of their daily efforts to navigate and manage perceptions of "sameness" while suppressing "difference" the field's entrenched whiteness, maleness, and middle-class bias will continue to undermine their careers.

The UK Black Comms (2024) report, *One Step Forward Two Steps Black*, showed the severity of ongoing issues in the UK communications industry, noting that:

- Four in five (82%) Black and Mixed-Black communications professionals continue to face microaggressions, such as indirect and subtle forms of racial discrimination, in the workplace;
- A significant 65% choose to ignore these microaggressions and racist comments;
- Over two-thirds (68%) of Black talent have considered leaving the public relations industry.

Pompper's (2005, 2013) perspective echoed these challenges faced by minority practitioners, emphasising that the industry's dominant culture often marginalises those who do not conform to established norms. In addition, Pompper (2013) specifically highlighted how diversity initiatives can sometimes inadvertently reinforce the very power structures they aim to dismantle, by failing to address the deeper systemic issues at play.

Dimensions of Diversity

Diversity is a broad concept that goes beyond race, encompassing multiple dimensions that enrich experiences and perspectives in any professional field and in society as a whole. The term "diversity" can be used to encompass religion, with its varied beliefs and practices; ethnicity, which encompasses cultural heritage and ethnic roots; and social class, which influences access to opportunities and resources. Gender identity and sexual orientation are also crucial aspects that affect both professional and personal life. Additionally, disability and neurodiversity require specific considerations to ensure an inclusive environment. Generational diversity, with its different perspectives and skills, along with geographical location, which brings regional and cultural differences, are also important. Finally, language and accent can significantly influence communication and perception in the workplace (Shen et al., 2009).

Building on this foundation, this section delves deeper into specific dimensions of diversity, such as ethnicity, religion, language, social class (and associated areas such as accent, location, and social capital), gender, neurodiversity, and disability as well as their links to social mobility. These areas were identified as key issues by the interviewees featured in Chapter 2. However, we also take the opportunity to explore other aspects of diversity, such as sexuality, which intersect with these dimensions in meaningful ways.

Understanding these various dimensions of diversity is essential in the field of public relations, as they directly impact representation and access to professional roles. Each dimension plays a critical role in shaping the experiences of practitioners and influencing the narratives constructed within the industry. Therefore, key aspects of diversity relevant to public relations include the following but it should be remembered that few dimensions can be considered in isolation and intersectionality should always be considered as many practitioners experience multiple layers of oppression (Applebaum, 2009).

Reading 1 The Business Case for Diversity

Read the extracts from the two interviews. While the two perspectives are broadly similar, can you note any points of difference between the two writers?

Extract from an interview with Lee Edwards: *Diversity in the PR Profession.* Retrieved from: https://www.lse.ac.uk/media-and-communications/research/MediaLSE-Long-Reads/Dr-Lee-Edwards-MediaLSE-Long-Reads-interview

What do you think the impact of the lack of diversity has on actual content production within the PR industry—are they able to put out content that is generally reflective of British society as a whole? Is there a real issue with content production just targeting certain audiences, or do you think practitioners can get over that regardless of their own personal backgrounds?

There has been some research in the U.S. by Vardeman-Winter et al. (2013) who talk about the need to have practitioners who understand the lives of their constituents, so that they can produce communication that actually works for those constituents, that relates to their concerns and interests. I think there's certainly a case for arguing that.

The other thing that you see in the strategic communications industries more broadly, because organisations are so insular and because they employ the same kind of person over and over again, is that they make horrendous mistakes around gender and race in particular that then create all sorts of crises that they have to manage reputationally. So, I think it is true that if you have a better understanding of the communities that you are dealing with and if you are able to in particular understand the lives that they lead and the pressures that they face and the context in which your communication is being received, then the chances are you'll produce the kind of communication that they're more likely to listen to.

I am really hesitant about the business case for diversity, though. The business case is this idea of matching your practitioner with the audience that you're supposed to be serving, and adding diversity to your own organisation, which enhances creativity, productivity and ultimately, the bottom line. The difficulty then is that diversity becomes disposable. If your business changes the case for diversity disappears, or if an agency comes along that can replace your diverse in-house staff by delivering well-targeted campaigns, the rationale to improve in-house diversity is gone. And for me, that's a really dangerous position to take. You have to combine that very obvious utility of having somebody who understands your communities, with the moral case for employing a diverse range of people and broadening access to the professions.

References

Vardeman-Winter, J., Tindall, N., & Jiang, J. (2013). Intersectionality and publics: How exploring publics' multiple identities questions basic public relations concepts. *Public Relations Inquiry, 2*(3), 279–304.

Extract from an article by Melissa Lawrence, (former) chief executive of the Taylor Bennett Foundation: *Diversity is central to council communications teams' success. Here's how we can drive change.* Retrieved from: https://www.local.gov.uk/our-support/leadership-workforce-and-communications/comms-hub-communications-support/futurecomms-11

Diversity is central to council communications teams' success. Here's how we can drive change

The lack of diversity in the wider sector is echoed in council communications teams. The LGA's [Local Government Association] most recent Head of Communications survey revealed that just 3% of council Head of Communications were from non-white ethnic minority backgrounds.

A diverse workforce should be central to local councils at all levels—to be effective we should reflect the communities we serve. Diversity brings so much to the table; whether that's through thoughts, experience, ideas, or insights. If you have a diverse community, you need that reflected in your teams. If you don't have an understanding or insight of a variety of experiences and cultures, it won't translate into the services your council delivers or the products you produce.

Especially in terms of communications. How can you expect to speak to your communities and residents if there's no variety of experience, background and skills? I always think of Hackney Council [the local authority for the London Borough of Hackney, in Greater London, UK] as a great example. The work they do for the community and the way they communicate with their residents, whether that's through their production of the Hackney Carnival or their support for the Windrush generation [people who moved to the UK from Commonwealth countries in the Caribbean between 1948 and 1971], feels authentic and genuine. The Hackney Carnival in particular feels that way to me—I have a Caribbean background. It speaks to so many people in that borough and it speaks to real lived experience. That's the power of effective communications.

We've gotten really good at talking about diversity, but we're not acting to level the playing field. There are many things that we can do as communicators in local government to change this, so that people from minority backgrounds can get and keep the jobs they want, and equally so council communication teams can reap the benefits of a variety of cultures and experiences.

Ethnicity

An ethnic group is made up of individuals who share a common cultural heritage, which is often reflected in their language and religious practices. Ethnicity encompasses various aspects, including language, religion, and other cultural factors shared among groups of people (Ertem-Eray & Ki, 2021; Konrad et al., 2006). Bilge et al. (2021) argued that although the concept of ethnicity is associated with culture, nationality, group, or identity, much of the academic literature in the field of communication conceptualises ethnicity primarily from a cultural perspective, highlighting how shared cultural practices and beliefs are transmitted through a process of socialisation that can fix culture to an individual or group.

Ethnicity has been a topic of discussion in organisational literature and we can trace its recognition as a topic of interest in public relations theory and research to over two decades ago as issues related to increasing ethnic diversity in the workforce began to be recognised. Organisational studies revealed that while companies responded positively to market diversity, there was a lack of commitment to integrating ethnic diversity internally (e.g., Bridgen, 2024; Diggs-Brown & Zaharna, 1995). Diggs-Brown & Zaharna (1995) found that many organisations in the U.S. context lacked adequate programmes for the retention and recruitment of ethnic minority employees, reflecting a low responsiveness to their specific needs.

In the field of public relations, academic literature has largely focused on cultural issues related to ethnicity while practice-based studies tend to discuss recruitment, retention, progression and the value of diversity. Pompper (2007) noted that ethnicity is closely linked to culture. Organisational cultures can perpetuate discrimination against ethnic minorities affecting their status, employment, and access to resources. Similarly, Abdullah (2007) emphasised that a proper understanding of aspects such as language, religious rituals, and taboos can reduce conflicts and enhance organisational performance. Furthermore, Abdullah stressed that public relations professionals need to be sensitive to local cultures and communicate in their clients' languages to avoid misunderstandings and foster more effective relationships in international contexts. This perspective underscores the importance of critically examining how cultural practices within organisations can influence the representation and treatment of employees from different ethnic backgrounds.

Religion

There has been little academic writing on religion as an aspect of diversity within the public relations profession, even though there is a body of literature on the use of public relations to promote particular faiths (e.g., Smith, 2020; Tilson & Venkateswaran, 2006; Xifra, 2008). However, Smudde (2021) acknowledged the importance of faith within the workplace, observing that a quarter century of scholarship has revealed the prominent role of spirituality and religion in the workplace.

Most writing that links public relations practice to the religious beliefs of practitioners is from professional rather than academic publications, where faith and religion are recorded as something exceptional rather than the norm. Parallels can be drawn with CRT, where the UK's dominant Christian religion and its associated social mores are viewed as normal and natural, whereas other forms of belief are often held up for their "difference." For example, articles in magazines, such as PR Week, call on practitioners to engage with Islamic communities (e.g., Dhunna, 2019; Hassan, 2018), often aiming to foster better communication. However, there are few articles in PR Week addressing other religions (including Christianity) and, likewise, few that discuss the issues faced by practitioners who openly practise their own faith. Nonetheless, there are exceptions, such as Barrett (2024), who addresses these issues explicitly.

Language

Language is fundamental for facilitating communication between individuals. It is conceptualised as a system of sentences, each of which has a finite length and is constructed from a limited set of basic elements (Chomsky, 1957, p. 13, as cited in Ertem-Eray & Ki, 2021). In the context of public relations, language plays a crucial role in how interactions are perceived and understood. Linguistic diversity reflects different cultural backgrounds and can influence communication dynamics, highlighting the importance of recognising and valuing these differences in interactions (Hideg et al., 2024).

In organisational settings, while linguistic diversity can enrich team dynamics and foster an inclusive environment, it also presents challenges related to effective communication and mutual understanding. If these challenges are not recognised and addressed, they can create significant obstacles to realising the benefits of integration within the workplace (Kim et al., 2019). For instance, many Black public relations professionals feel compelled to modify their language to conform to dominant social norms. A recent study, commissioned by the UK Black Comms Network (2024), revealed that 66% of Black and mixed-race public relations professionals in the UK reported engaging in "code-switching," altering their behaviour, accent, or language to avoid discrimination and meet workplace expectations. This underscores the pressures minority groups face in striving to maintain their authentic voices in professional settings.

Furthermore, research on language in the public relations industry highlighted its critical role in shaping perceptions of diversity. Austin (2010) noted that various articles emphasise how organisations articulate diversity internally and in their communications with diverse stakeholders. However, strict adherence to certain style guides can inadvertently offend some communities, especially when disparities exist in how different racial groups are represented.

Social Class and Its Relationship to Accent, Location and Social Capital

The concept of class is somewhat "fuzzy" because it serves both as a specific way of interpreting economic inequalities and as a simplified representation of these inequalities (Anthias, 2001). Class can be explored, for instance, via the consumption of cultural products with emphasis placed on cultural values (e.g., Warde et al., 1999), ways of life, taste and social preference, and the creation of social distance.

Anthias (2013) observed that writing on class has tended to be focused on the "understandings of white actors," creating a subtext where lifestyle, image, and identity issues for white individuals pertain to class rather than ethnicity. In contrast, similar forms of embodiment that articulate status and deference for minority or racialised populations are often viewed through the lens of race or ethnic constructions rather than class (p. 124). This suggests that the experience of social class, particularly from the perspective of race or other forms of disadvantage such as disability, are under-theorised.

Accent is an intrinsic feature of language as it plays a crucial role in how speech is perceived and understood. Variations in accent often reflect diverse linguistic and cultural backgrounds.

Linguistic diversity can have a significant impact on communication and perception and; as Randle et al. (2015) outlined, "[a]ccent [is] seen as an important signifier of the possession (or otherwise) of the 'right' cultural capital for engaging successfully in the sector" (p. 598). The authors also noted that some media workers interviewed felt that certain accents were associated with lower levels of intelligence.

Although organisations are increasingly hiring individuals who work in a non-native language or those who speak the same language but have diverse accents (Kim et al., 2019), prejudice still exists. Academic literature on the effects of accent on recruitment and progression in the public relations industry is sparse; however, there is more work on the impact of accent in media industries (Randle et al., 2015). In contrast, reports from a practice-based perspective, such as those by the Black Comms Network (2024), are more prevalent.

Gender

Gender, which refers to the socially constructed roles and behaviours associated with biological sex, shapes societal norms and influences expectations for men and women (Ertem-Eray & Ki, 2021, p. 3). These gender constructs significantly impact both personal and professional experiences, influencing how individuals navigate the workplace and how organisations develop their cultures and policies.

The importance of addressing gender diversity in public relations is underscored by numerous studies that highlight the need for awareness of gender issues within organisations (e.g., Fine et al., 2020; Halford, 2018; Tindall & Waters, 2012). Despite women being predominant in the public relations industry and academia there is a notable underrepresentation of gender-based research and any acknowledgement of the personal narratives of women in the field—in particular from an intersectional standpoint. As Vardeman-Winter and Place (2017) stressed, "women's stories—as well as those of men who do not fit the standard White, heterosexual, American experience—are severely underrepresented in public relations practice and research" (p. 326). This lack of diverse representation demonstrates the need for storytelling that reflects a broader range of experiences and perspectives.

Moreover, the field of public relations continues to grapple with patriarchal gender relations that influence its dynamics (e.g., Fröhlich and Peters (2007)). These entrenched norms impact the industry's struggle for academic legitimacy and professional recognition (Fitch & Third, 2010). Although women constitute a significant portion of the workforce, patriarchal structures persist, hindering genuine equality and diversity.

Authors like Al-Jenaibi (2011) argued that the public relations industry should cultivate a culture that integrates and respects diverse gender narratives. By doing so, it can more effectively serve the diverse societies it aims to represent and enhance its role as a communicator of inclusive and authentic narratives. Furthermore, Al-Jenaibi (2011, p. 51), suggested that efforts to promote gender diversity should focus on diversifying work styles and encouraging cooperation between genders, particularly in regions like the United Arab Emirates (UAE), where such initiatives can drive positive change.

Neurodiversity and Dis/ability

While there is a considerable body of knowledge on the representation of disability in the media (e.g., Cumberbatch and Negrine (2022); Geothals et al (2022)) and the use of public relations techniques to promote—for instance, disability rights (e.g., Trevisan, 2017) and disability sport (e.g., De Haan et al., 2015)—, there remains a significant gap in literature regarding public relations practitioners with disabilities. The CIPR's report, *PR Population Report*, indicated that 8% of practitioners consider themselves to have a disability, with most reporting that their disability limits them only slightly (Chartered Institute of Public Relations, 2022a).

Although research exists on the experiences of individuals with disabilities in professions such as law (White et al., 2021) and teaching (Anderson, 2006), there is a lack of writing on the lived experiences of disabled public relations practitioners, as well as theories and research addressing their challenges. Additionally, while there is an increasing amount of professional writing in this area, it often revolves on first-person accounts and case studies (e.g., Bassil, 2024; Kim, 2021), neglecting broader issues of integration and intersectionality because disability can also intersect with other factors such as race, social class, and age, impacting a practitioner's ability to advance or remain in their role—a crucial omission. Nonetheless, there is a growing body of professional literature focused on creating diverse and accessible workplaces for individuals with disabilities (e.g., Rawat, 2023; White-Sax, 2024; Williams, 2023).

White et al. (2021) pointed out that legal practitioners with disabilities provide valuable insider perspectives and may assist others with disabilities to participate in court systems, potentially ensuring access to justice for a wider range of individuals. The authors also underlined that law professionals with disabilities can recommend effective communication methods and strategies.

Generational Diversity

Research by the Chartered Institute of Public Relations (2024) report revealed that only 8% of public relations practitioners were over the age of 55. However, age diversity concerns all age groups—a practitioner can face discrimination for being perceived as either too young or too old for a certain role. Despite a recognised skills shortage in the industry, older professionals are often underrepresented, either due to exclusion from recruitment or having left the profession. As Flegg (2022) observed:

> I would contend that the underrepresentation of older age groups in our profession is an issue contributed to by ageism in recruitment and talent development practices inside and outside organisations. And yes, that includes using particular words in job adverts.
>
> (par. 18)

While there are guidelines on creating and fostering age-diverse workplaces (e.g. Haynes, 2011; Benfield, 2019), there is limited guidance or leadership from those in senior positions. Shen and Jiang (2013) are among the few scholars who have explored generational diversity in public relations, although their research mainly focused on work-life balance among different age groups. They mentioned that "[i]nvestigating how each generation experiences work-life conflict has significant implications for employers and employees to better understand and handle important issues including career management, teamwork, leadership, communication, job satisfaction, child bearing, child rearing, and marital and family satisfaction" (p. 75).

Meanwhile, academic writing on generational diversity, particularly its intersections with other forms of diversity, in the field of public relations remains limited. However, scholarship on age in other occupations is abundant, covering a wide range of perspectives, such as job satisfaction (Dello Russo et al, 2021; Mottaz, 1987) and beliefs about ageing (Weiss et al., 2022).

Sexuality

Sexuality is another intricate aspect of diversity within the public relations profession. The literature on sexual orientation and public relations remains limited, despite the fact that, according to the Chartered Institute of Public Relations' (2024) report, around 10% of public relations practitioners identify as lesbian, gay, bisexual, or any other non-heterosexual sexual orientation, compared to 7% in other professional sectors. As Tindall and Waters (2012) pointed out, "[d]espite the increasing focus on understanding the diversity of public relations, academics and practitioners have largely ignored gay men" (p. 451). Writing from a queer theory perspective, Tindall and Waters argued:

> [m]embers of this community are commonly linked together under the umbrella terms of gay and LGBTQ+ (for lesbian, gay, bisexual, and transgender), yet that is a false universalization that purports that all members are perceived as equal and that all members share and have the same experiences.
>
> (p. 452)

Thus, it is essential to recognise the intersectionality inherent in such experience.

Ciszek (2018) highlighted a growth in scholarship on this subject, though much of it has focused on public relations campaigns and activism rather than the experience of LGBTQ+ individuals working within the industry. She observed that "[a]lthough a handful of studies have dabbled in queer theory (e.g., Cabosky, 2014; Edwards & L'Etang, 2013; Mundy, 2015; Tindall & Waters, 2012), a comprehensive theoretical foundation has not been laid for building queer inquiry in public relations" (p. 3). Nevertheless, more recently, scholars like Ciszek (2018) began to expand the field, exploring the lived experiences of gay practitioners of colour.

Practitioners' studies have moved beyond simply quantifying and recording sexual orientation data. A CIPR's 2024 study emphasised the challenges which can occur when individuals feel compelled to downplay or hide their sexuality:

> Not feeling able to be authentic can take a toll on people's wellbeing and belonging. When people choose to 'come out', some highlighted negative experiences of discrimination and exclusion in the workplace in relation to their LGBTQ+ identity. Lesbian, gay, bisexual and queer people are significantly more likely than heterosexual professionals to experience several types of discrimination.
>
> (Bell, 2024, p. 47)

Defining Social Mobility in the Context of Public Relations

The Creative Industries Policy and Evidence Centre (2021) observed massive class-based disadvantage in the creative sector. However, despite much discussion in the public relations industry about the need to improve "social mobility" and "diversity," both terms are rarely defined within the discipline. Their meanings are often assumed, leading to potential misunderstandings. Drawing from the work of Brook et al. (2018), we recognise the confusion surrounding the meaning of "social mobility," where in public policy it addresses a raft of social issues associated with inequality in the UK (Social Mobility Commission, 2022); in academic contexts, it refers more precisely and technically to shifts in social structure as well as individual life chances.

As this book draws from both practical and academic research, including interviews with practitioners, there is a risk of blurring definitions. To avoid confusion, we have deliberately chosen to adopt a clear, social science definition: "[t]he movement in time of individuals, families, or other social units between positions of varying advantage in the system of social stratification of a society" (Müller & Pollak, 2015, p. 640). The public relations industry has acknowledged the lack of social mobility, particularly as the proportion of privately educated practitioners continues to rise although as Baird and Bridgen (2023) observed, the industry is not innovative in its recruitment practices and does not see diversity and inclusion as an industry focus. Furthermore, they noted that any industry focus on improving social mobility tends to overlook geographical disadvantage and when intersected with other factors such as race, gender and social class, this means that some practitioners suffer multiple disadvantages.

Training Programmes Designed to Increase Diversity in Public Relations

There are a number of training initiatives within the field of public relations and communications which aim to give Black, Asian, and ethnic minority and other practitioners from underrepresented groups the skills, knowledge, and contacts necessary to succeed in a field predominantly occupied by white, middle-class and privately educated practitioners (Chartered Institute of Public Relations, 2022b). However, as Bourne (2022), drawing on Ahmed (2012), pointed out, diversity initiatives can often act as symbolic gestures rather than effecting structural change. Ahmed critiqued these institutional commitments, noting that they may be considered "non-performatives" because they "do not bring into effect that which they name" (Ahmed, 2012, p. 119).

In this sense, Ahmed's concept of "non-performatives" suggested that diversity initiatives in the UK public relations sector may be little more than "public relations for public relations," where surface-level changes are made without addressing deeper systemic issues (Bourne, 2022). Gregory (2022, p. 401) also stressed that the industry "does not open its doors, make welcome, reward or honour its own diverse community." This reflects what has been described as called "racial capitalism" (Hammer, 2023), where diversity discourses are commodified for reputational gain, instead of challenging the industry's structural inequalities. Furthermore, Bourne argued that such initiatives reproduce whiteness by requiring racialised public relations professionals to conform to white gatekeepers' expectations, perpetuating racial hierarchies rather than dismantling them. Nonetheless, those who are graduates of courses are usually positive about the experience (as we will see in Chapter 2) and look beyond these issues at the career benefits and social capital that these programmes give them.

Conclusion

This book adds to the literature on race, diversity, and social mobility by firstly reviewing and analysing the current research and thinking in these areas, and secondly grounding these themes in the lived experiences of public relations practitioners. Through these narratives, it aims to provide points for discussion and throws light on the discrimination faced by practitioners while also offering a platform for reflection and dialogue. By intertwining theory with personal stories, we aspire to encourage both practitioners and academics to critically explore their own practice and engage in meaningful conversations of these complex topics with others. Chapter 2 particularly aims to bring the challenges faced by practitioners to light and shows how their opinions shaped by their lived experience bring to light the theory and research discussed in this chapter.

2 Using the Lived Experiences of Public Relations Practitioners to Explore Themes around Race, Diversity, and Social Mobility

This chapter explores the themes of race and social mobility in public relations through the lens of 11 interviews with British public relations practitioners who exhibit characteristics of diversity plus additional observations from practice-based literature. These in-person interviews, characterised by the directness and spontaneity recommended by Ortí (2010), offered a window into the diverse experiences of practitioners in the field. By connecting these narratives to the theoretical and research foundations discussed in Chapter 1, this chapter bridges personal lived experiences with broader academic discussions on diversity.

The practitioners were recruited through our networks and extended connections, as well as through collaboration with the administrators and managers of the industry training programmes mentioned below. This approach aimed to capture a broad representation of the diverse nature of British public relations professionals although we acknowledge that this representation is not complete, a point which is expanded upon below.

The training programmes selected for this research, and who allowed access to their students and graduates, vary in their scope and level of investment. One is focused on helping Black, Asian, and ethnic minority background individuals secure their first role in public relations, while another aimed to increase the representation of a wide range of minority practitioners in senior roles. These initiatives, operating at different levels, collectively highlight the efforts being made to address structural barriers and promote diversity within the public relations profession and are:

- Taylor Bennett Foundation PR training programme: This UK-based intensive course, run in partnership with leading public relations agencies, is designed to help Black, Asian, and ethnic minority background graduates transition into public relations. It provides training and mentoring opportunities to increase diversity in the public relations industry (Taylor Bennett Foundation, n.d.).
- Socially Mobile: This programme delivers training to individuals from lower socio-economic backgrounds as well as underrepresented

DOI: 10.4324/9781032692234-3

> and under-served groups including ethnic minority practitioners, the LGBTQ+ community, women returners, and those with disabilities. (Socially Mobile, n.d.).

Meanwhile, other interviewees were recruited through author networks—via social media platforms such as LinkedIn, a private Facebook group for public sector professionals, and personal contact—and shared how they had forged their own unique paths into public relations. Their stories added depth and nuance to the exploration of race and social mobility in the field.

The interviews conducted can be viewed through multiple lenses and used to demonstrate the challenges faced by minority practitioners. Key issues identified included unconscious bias, which was present from the earliest stages of the recruitment process and in the workplace, as well as the lack of a "network" and how this impacted on choices available and the need to adjust behaviours to succeed in a white and masculine environment. These challenges were experienced in unique ways depending on the intersection of the practitioners' identities and backgrounds.

A recurring theme was the significant intersectionality which defines the lived reality for many practitioners. For instance, one interviewee, who identified as working class, Black, and from a region of the UK far removed from metropolitan public relations elites, illustrated how overlapping identities compounded their experiences of marginalisation. Others found it difficult to articulate precisely why or how they encountered discrimination though those based outside major cities often expressed feeling multiple layers of difference between themselves and their peers.

The interviews, conducted online via Microsoft Teams or Zoom between late 2023 and early 2024, were designed to ensure accessibility for participants regardless of geographical location. However, recruiting interviewees presented an ethical dilemma, as participants were asked to share their time and expertise—and potentially discuss sensitive or deeply personal topics—without compensation. The issue of unpaid labour is widely debated within the creative industries (e.g., Cohen, 2016; Hesmondhalgh & Baker, 2013), particularly among practitioners of colour, who often feel it is not their responsibility to "educate" white colleagues about their experiences for free (e.g., Eddo-Lodge, 2020).

These ethical considerations were carefully weighed during the recruitment and interview process, and we are profoundly thankful to the practitioners interviewed who generously shared their time and valuable insights, offering a candid glimpse into their lives and work-related challenges. In addition, we are grateful to the administrators of the training programmes mentioned above for giving us access to their students and graduates. To minimise bias, the recruitment strategy intentionally avoided involving individuals personally known to us to avoid any "groupthink" that can result from interviewing small samples of people belonging to social cliques and networks or who share a geographical location (Halrynjo & Lyng, 2009). By diversifying the participant pool, we aimed to capture a broader spectrum of experiences and prevent the repetition of homogenous narratives across interviews.

The interviews were recorded and transcribed with the transcription accompanied by observation notes. Data analysis was carried out using Atlas.ti version 24.1.1 software, following the steps outlined in Townsend (2003). The interviews were conducted around a range of themes rather than a series of questions—an unstructured interview style which was also conversational. This use of conversation as a research methodology is rooted in the interpretivist paradigm, which posits that reality is socially constructed and can be understood through the interpretation of human interactions (Bryman, 2016). It allowed the interviewer to build a rapport with the subject and, while this research approach does not attempt to produce a framework or model (which would be impossible anyway) it uses a phenomenological approach to increase understanding of an issue within the lived experience of the practitioners interviewed.

Self-Identification of Participants

The interviewees were allowed to define their own identities rather than having labels assigned. The responses highlighted the diversity and complexity of personal identities, showing the wide range of intersectionalities that exist among public relations practitioners in the UK. For example, one participant described themselves as "white British, middle-aged and dyslexic" (interviewee 11), while another identified as "white, binary" (interviewee 4), showcasing how individuals perceive and express their identities and identify categories which mattered to them. Interestingly, not all white practitioners defined themselves as such, reflecting the perception that whiteness is the norm (Jensen, 2021).

Other participants identified themselves using multiple descriptors that encompassed aspects of race, ethnicity, and cultural background For instance, one interviewee said, "I class myself as um, Afro Caribbean stroke, uh, Black, [UK region] or Black British" (Interviewee 2), highlighting a nuanced understanding of racial and cultural identity, while another noted, "mixed race, so my mum is from [Western Europe] and my dad was from [East Africa)]" (Interviewee 6), illustrating the intersectionality of race and ethnicity. Furthermore, some participants emphasised their cultural or religious affiliations, such as being a "cultural Muslim, not a practising Muslim, but a Muslim nonetheless" (Interviewee 9), or identifying as a "Black Christian woman" (Interviewee 8), which underscores the role of faith and culture in shaping their identities (Table 2.1). This range of responses illustrates the diverse ways individuals perceive and articulate their identities, challenging simplistic labels and highlighting the importance of allowing individuals to define themselves on their own terms.

Table 2.1 Self-Identification of interviewees

Identifier	*Self-identity*
1	Male, young, lower middle class, regional UK city (north)
2	Male, working class, Black, regional UK city (north)
3	Female, working class, middle aged, regional UK city (midlands)
4	Female, white, middle class (working class parents), London
5	Female, working class, regional UK city (north)
6	Female, mixed race, working class, London
7	Female, working class, cisgender, middle aged, regional UK city (north)
8	Female, young, Black, London
9	Female, middle aged, working class, Asian, "cultural Muslim," regional UK city (north)
10	Male, middle aged, working class, Pakistani background, regional UK city (north)
11	Female, middle aged, middle class, disability, UK region (midlands)

Note: Each interviewee was given a number as an identifier.

Social class was also self-identified by participants, often based on their parents' jobs, educational background, or personal achievements. Many interviewees described themselves as coming from a working-class background, with statements such as "I grew up in a very working-class background" (Interviewee 9), reflecting their socio-economic roots. In addition, several interviewees emphasised being the first in their family to attend university, marking a significant milestone in their social mobility and potentially highlighting their working-class origins. Others expressed a more nuanced view of class, with one participant stating, "Middle class—father from a working-class background but went to university" (Interviewee 4), indicating a complex nature of class identity that often includes elements of both working and middle-class backgrounds and the role of education in defining social class. In contrast, some interviewees identified as "lower middle class" (e.g., Interviewee 1) reflecting personal perceptions of class linked to financial independence, lifestyle, and responsibilities. This tendency to focus on socio-economic factors over other dimensions of identity highlights how social norms shape and influence self-identification, especially among white participants.

Thematics Identified in the Interviews

In this chapter, the thematic areas identified in the interviews provide an opportunity to explore the intersections of race, diversity, and social mobility within the public relations. The discussions, guided by the interviewer but shaped by the individual experiences of practitioners, highlight the issues they find of relevance and importance. Each interviewee had the freedom to direct the conversation towards the themes that resonated with their own experiences, shedding light on the complexities of these topics in the context of their careers and professional lives.

The interviewees raised a wide variety of themes and the focus of this chapter is on the seven most commonly occurring themes which are categorised as follows into two main strands:

Strand 1: Diversity and Discrimination

- Race and identity
- Understanding the benefits and advantages of diversity through lived experiences
- Discrimination in the industry: how it is manifested
- Recruitment, promotion and everyday life

Strand 2: Access and Impact of Initiatives Designed to Encourage Diversity in Public Relations

- Access to initiatives and experiences of programmes
- Impact on career
- Impact on social mobility

Strand 1: Diversity and Discrimination

Diversity, as discussed in Chapter 1, is inherently subjective and constantly evolving, and it is inevitable that the participants would each understand diversity from their own life experience, academic knowledge, and practice-based learning. Yet, diversity is often accompanied by forms of discrimination and unequal access to opportunities in the workplace; as was highlighted by one of the interviewees:

> I think sometimes it's about people not being offered the same opportunities for not just the career progression in terms of there's a role that you could consider blind [blinded applications—not seeing name, gender etc. on applications] for, but where's the training and development opportunities?
>
> (Interviewee 10)

This strand examines diversity and discrimination from multiple perspectives: how race and identity influence practitioners' experiences, how the benefits of diversity are understood and leveraged, and how discrimination manifests at various levels, from hiring practices to workplace culture. Through these insights, the strand reveals the challenges of fostering an equitable profession while highlighting opportunities for growth.

Race and Identity

An individual's identity is core to an individual's understanding of who they are. These characteristics shape each person's experiences, relationships, and opportunities throughout their lives. Most of the interviewees were proud of many aspects of their identity and sought acknowledgement of it in the workplace. As we have shown above, practitioners from ethnic minorities saw this as part of their identities yet white practitioners did not always feel it relevant to share such details. While scholars such as Logan (2011) observed that this is because white culture is seen as the norm and therefore not a matter of identification many of the interviewees identified the need to express identity as a way of foregrounding overlooked people:

> Black History Month as to something we've done [at my workplace] because you know, our culture celebrates this month for a reason. It's because Black culture has been side-lined, has been marginalised and to kind of dismiss it as just an event that [...] we don't really have to worry about [is wrong].
>
> (Interviewee 9)

Identity was also used to identify discrimination and industry issues as this quote demonstrates:

> Certainly the people I know from ethnically diverse backgrounds working in our industry work really hard because they feel they have to and I very rarely know of people from diverse backgrounds who don't commit to working above their contracted hours.
>
> (Interviewee 10)

The Director of Diversity and Inclusion at the University of Wolverhampton, Adam Vasco (2024), observed that those from a diverse background often feel pressurised by society—or colleagues—into being a spokesperson for that group or to understand or be able to explain issues facing them. It is important to remember that the "burden of 'representing' a whole demographic is rarely placed on white leaders" (Vasco 2024, par. 4) Vasco also suggests that viewing diverse leaders in terms of what they can do for their particular group diminishes their other skills and attributes.

The interviews revealed a distinction between those identities which could be deliberately concealed—such as certain disabilities, accents, and aspects of social class—and immutable characteristics, particularly race, that could not be hidden. Conversely, Interviewee 11 explained why, in her opinion, it was not always beneficial to conceal certain identities and how concealment can perpetuate discrimination:

> [My dyslexia] hasn't been too much of a problem. I don't always disclose I'm dyslexic. Well, so when I started, you didn't obviously have [...] protected characteristics [enshrined in law]. So, you know, my concern would

> be [that] if I said I am dyslexic, then it's like well, "you can't do comms", but now, you know, I would disclose it because it does (mean I) think differently or approach things differently sometimes.

Those with immutable identities believed that their possession of protected characteristics often resulted in discrimination, though proving such discrimination in the workplace could be a challenge, as we will discuss below.

Furthermore, social class frequently intersected with race, adding further layers of disadvantage to practitioners from ethnic minorities. This can lead to additional discrimination as Interviewee 3 observed when considering how in UK society greater value is based on some universities over others. She also observed that, as a person from a working class background, she was unaware that employers would place different values on different universities—something that a middle class person would automatically be aware of. She made this discovery only when looking for her first job.

> [...] Basically for the first sift, if you haven't been to one of those universities you were put in like a kind of reject pile to be looked at again later if [they] didn't have enough numbers from that first first and maybe have a second tier as well, which they'd go to next and then everyone else.
>
> (Interviewee 3)

The impact of race and identity at all stages of a person's education and working life cannot be underestimated. How a person identifies themselves can affect their access to ideas, opportunities and networks but even if they are able to access these, they may be judged or rejected because of who they are (Banerjee, 2013).

Understanding the Benefits and Advantages of Diversity Through Lived Experiences

Jones et al. (2020) and Jackson and Joshi (2004) argued that diversity in teams encompasses not only varied backgrounds but also a diversity of thought and perspective. This richness in viewpoints strengthens teams by bringing innovative and creative solutions to complex issues.

Interviewee 8 highlighted the importance of public relations and communications teams reflecting the diverse stakeholders they serve:

> 90% of the PR industry is white. So [...] are they truly reflecting being paid to deliver on campaigns, on all forms of work to meet a society or to meet the audiences that may be diverse? How do you truly meet those briefs if you do not reflect being the society, the audience, that the company wants to serve?

Interviewee 4 shared a nuanced example:

> People assume that Eid [one of the biggest celebrations in the Islamic calendar] is like Christmas and it's one day. [I] remember having this conversation and explaining to them (people at work) that it's more along ethnicity lines. So actually this year [2023] was an exception where everyone had Eid on the same day, but most years people from the Middle East [...] follow the Saudis and they usually [celebrate Eid] a day earlier than people from South Asia.

Nevertheless, as we have seen in Chapter One, diversity transcends understanding client demographics, though that remains important and equally, as explained above, it is not the responsibility of a practitioner from a minority group to represent others who share their characteristics. Despite this, as Edwards (2014a, 2023) and Bourne (2022) observed, a lack of diversity often leads to replicating a white, male norm of management throughout organisations, stifling creativity and disadvantaging individuals from minority backgrounds who do not "fit" in with the organisation. Edwards (2013) and Carbado (2013) argued that whiteness, maleness, and middle-class standards are normalised in public relations practice and therefore invisible.

> Diversity is so important for diversity of thought—often teams think [...] one way—for instance at the start of lockdown, not realising that not everyone had the internet at home or home wasn't always a safe place. People from secure backgrounds don't always realise this.
>
> (Interviewee 4)

> You've got those diverse perspectives, so it can just encourage greater ideas and innovation.
>
> (Interviewee 6)

> It's about culture isn't it really? So for me, like culture in the organisation, if you're being chair (e.g. of a meeting), you see everyone around that board table looked the exact same and they're just paying lip service to EDI and, you know, yeah, it's so obvious because they're not doing [diversity] work.
>
> (Interviewee 7)

Further themes were explored such as the value of mentorship in supporting diversity. Interviewee 22 questioned whether the mentors and coaches recommended by professional associations genuinely serve individuals from diverse backgrounds, emphasising that a focus on diversity alone is insufficient. In this context, Interviewee 10 observed:

> I think the challenge isn't the diversity [...] it's the career progression that comes with it. Where are your leaders and why are we still [like] this?

> What feels like a diverse environment [is not diverse if it is] not able to produce senior level communicators and senior level professionals in other functions as well.

The Chartered Institute of Public Relations (2024) report substantiated this concern, revealing that only a small percentage of practitioners in senior leadership positions are from ethnic minority backgrounds. This lack of representation is a serious issue, as noted by Interviewee 10, who expressed frustration at being one of the few senior communications leaders from an ethnically diverse background in the north of England.

> Sometimes I'm embarrassed when I look around and see myself as one of the most senior communicators from an ethnically diverse background in [large public sector organisation].

Interviewee 10 also pointed out the scarcity of diverse representation in senior roles in the public relations industry, not only among people from ethnically diverse backgrounds but also among individuals with disabilities and women. For those who embody multiple facets of diversities, the issue of representation becomes even more pressing.

Discrimination in the Industry: How It Is Manifested

While not every participant reported direct discrimination or perceived personal experiences of it, many stressed indirect forms of discrimination and a general lack of awareness about how to communicate effectively with the UK's diverse population. This aligns with the work of Edwards' (2014b), who demonstrated how the industry's discourse can create barriers to diversity by "ignoring or problematising marginalised identities, denying the existence of discrimination and reifying merit" (p. 329). Therefore, discrimination often surfaced not through overt actions, but in the absence of representation and opportunities. For instance, Interviewee 10 highlighted the lack of diversity in senior roles:

> In terms of diversity, [what] have we got? A diverse group of colleagues in comms, most of them are [...] Muslim. In terms of salary bands these people] probably stop at Band 6 or Band 7 [specialist and middle management salary grades] and so where are your more senior communicators?

This underrepresentation has implications in terms of career aspirations. Thus, Interviewee 3 explained that it was "very hard to imagine myself in that [management] kind of role."

For individuals who did aim for promotion, barriers often remained. For example, Interviewee 8 expressed frustration over a lack of accountability and true commitment to diversity in the workplace:

> The office was not truly prepared systemically and psychologically for change. It was more about, well, let's see if we can try this again, but there was no real intention from management and senior leadership to really hold people accountable.

In addition to the lack of accountability and true commitment, Interviewee 8 also pointed out that bullying and exclusion were pervasive issues within the workplace. The participant detailed how a coach obstructed professional advancement: "My coach gate-kept opportunities [from me] and sabotaged my opportunity to move to another office [...]. Told me to my face that if I'm not gonna work here, I won't work anywhere." This experience not only had a significant impact on the interviewee's mental health, but also was symptomatic of a toxic workplace environment where bullying thrived, and silence became a defensive mechanism against subtle violence and fear of reprisals:

> All of this was so mentally overwhelming because it's happening in real time, but you still have to show up and perform. Even though your colleagues know something's not, something isn't right here, but everyone's afraid to say something.
>
> (Interviewee 8)

It was clear that white, working-class, practitioners also experienced discrimination but this manifested itself in different ways. It is important to stress that a working-class background can become less relevant or hidden as a career progresses—on the outside at least—something that is not an option for those from an evident racial background. Working class practitioners interviewed often felt they lacked social capital necessary to initiate or advance their careers.

> For every reason, the right door took a while to open, and I truly believe that some of that's down to connections, and yet the ability to present yourself.
>
> (Interviewee 10)

They perceived "connections"—themselves hard to define—as a significant barrier, along with their performative expectations tied to social class. Being able to behave in the same way as the majority was seen as crucial. This led to a lack of confidence in their abilities, something which will be developed further in findings around training programmes and progression.

This intersectionality highlights the complex dynamics of race, identity, and social class, suggesting that merely having a diverse workforce is insufficient without addressing the underlying structures that sustain inequality.

In addition, conversations with interviewees showed that an accent—a badge of someone's class and location for practitioners in the UK—had a huge impact on recruitment, progression, and job satisfaction. Accent can be a sole factor in discrimination but is often linked to other factors—such as ethnicity and disability. Essentially, the interviewees described below demonstrated that a white, middle-class norm was present through recruitment and progression and strong regional accents were discriminated against. The interviewees became conscious of their accent and felt as though it was a tool for discrimination as can be shown in the quotes below:

> When I worked at the Council I was told to take elocution lessons, and when I saw everyone [doing]other jobs getting promoted and I wasn't promoted and they were all sort of privately educated and stuff. […] I even looked for jobs in London and I was down at 10 Downing St. [official residence of the UK Prime Minister] for a job interview and I just felt like people looked down upon me because I had an accent.
>
> (Interviewee 5)

> [Because of] where I've been born and raised geographically my accent [goes against me]. [When] I am in [UK region] that kind of goes in my favour, but you know, working outside of [UK region] and probably more nationally [it] has kind of gone against me.
>
> (Interviewee 2)

> They didn't recruit someone because they [management] said "we work with a lot of international clients and they wouldn't understand them." But they just had a strong regional accent! They were Scottish, actually.
>
> (Interviewee 3)

Research by the UK Black Comms Network (2024) revealed that 66% of Black communications professionals felt that they had to "code-switch" in the workplace in order to fit in with their colleagues. The study showed that the need to modify accent and behaviour to "fit in" and remain employable and promotable was an additional challenge put upon all minority practitioners.

Reading 2 Explanation of Code-Switching. From the "One Step Forward Two Steps Black" Report Published by UK Black Comms Network, 2024

Code-switching involves consciously or unconsciously adjusting one's behaviour, accent, or language to conform to dominant social norms and prevent discrimination.

As of 2024, two-thirds (66%) of Black and Mixed Black PR professionals have had to code-switch when applying to roles in communications. Previous survey results indicate that 21% changed their voice or accent in 2022, and 33% did so in 2020. Additionally, 16% changed or shortened their names in 2022, compared to 21% in 2020.

A third (32%) reported altering their way of speaking, and a fifth (21%) reported changing their vocabulary to fit a workplace persona they felt compelled to adopt. Similarly, 30% felt they had to code-switch by modifying or concealing their personal experiences, interests, or characteristics to align with workplace conversations and social norms. Code-switching also affected visible characteristics: 10% reported changing their hairstyle, 9% changed their name, and 4% altered their style and physical appearance.

In addition, location—itself related to accent—can intersect with other forms of diversity to create multiple layers of discrimination. The public relations industry is largely concentrated in major metropolitan cities, and even with the move towards hybrid working, regular office attendance is still the norm. This puts pressure on those living outside urban centres who may find it challenging to relocate closer to a city centre workplace:

> [Large metropolitan city] is 30 miles down the road but transport and costs are just so bad it has never been a viable option until probably post pandemic, you know, a couple of days a week that would be doable.
>
> (Interviewee 1)

On the other hand, some interviewees felt that the industry lacked genuine commitment to change. This issue was highlighted by Interviewee 7, who said that "geographical issue in terms of access diversity is real, [and] that they [public relations leadership] don't seem to care about [it]." Furthermore, geography encompasses more than just physical location. The behaviours expected in the public relations landscape of major cities can also be seen as a barrier to entry. Not only are certain behaviours anticipated, but also specific standards of dress that vary across different work settings:

> When I started out, you know, there's a lot of kinds of black tie dinners and that kind of thing […] So then you have to go and buy loads of stuff that you haven't already got when you're not earning very much [… and now …] maybe there has been a bit of a change [...] PR has have kind of changed how they do some of their events and things, but that was quite a big one. You know if you expected to go and buy a dress sometimes like half your weekly salary.
>
> (Interviewee 3)

Tsetsura's (2012) observation that "practitioners reinforce […] professionalism by following dress codes in various work situations" (p. 15) is of interest given that public relations is still struggling to achieve legitimacy in many contexts (Gregory, 2020; Marschlich & Ingenhoff, 2021). As such, the emphasis on clothing is not only predictable, but also acts as a barrier for individuals from non-traditional backgrounds.

Reading 3 Extended Interview Extract: How Racism Is Experienced in the Workplace. Interviewee 8 Discusses her Experience

Interviewee 8: I don't think they [my employers] understood what diversity was. I think they understood it, but they didn't need to acknowledge it.

I've only had two major experiences [of work]: One in the UK working in [major metropolitan city] as a receptionist. [There] I think it was more of a class thing as opposed to a race thing, but there were a lot of intersections that compounded my experience there and at that time I was super young. I was like a receptionist for a PR agency trying to find my way to kind of break in [to the industry]. But that experience was just a reflection of [my view that] they don't want me to progress here. It's just a case that [the company] just wanted to showcase diversity but not really understanding the importance of that [and this was] one of the reasons why that experience was quite short lived. I think it was about a couple of weeks and then I just left because I didn't feel like I was being respected within the role. It was more of this is your title, so you're expected to do this. This, this and this as well. And yeah, I think because I was a minority out of the majority and there were no allies. It was very much a case of well, if I don't stand up for myself, who is? So I left.

And then [European city]. I think that's where the major lived experience came from [when I was] working for [a large PR consultancy]. I'd say the first six months was [viewed through] rose tinted glasses. Everybody was lovely, everybody was on their best behaviour. Everybody wanted to ensure that I was comfortable, but then it was like once everybody got comfortable, I got comfortable. The true outlooks, perceptions, questions, [and] education started and then that's when I realised that this company has not been prepared for diverse talent, but I'm also not a token or something you can put in a museum, which it very much then became much of to the point where I even experienced outside of work with the [European country] police. I was out with a colleague of mine, we're like sisters now, and she's white. She's from [Eastern Europe]. We went for a walk and then there was, like, a couple of police vans pulled up to us, took us apart, said to her like, you know, what are you doing with her? What are you doing walking on the road with her? And we were like what are you talking about? It was like it was in the middle of COVID where we were allowed to be out, taking walks and stuff because it was very strict in [country] what you could and couldn't do.

But you know, there's been a lot of experiences personally and professionally. [For instance] my coach gate-kept opportunities (from me) and sabotaged my opportunity to move to another office and go to the United States and open a digital practice. You know, they told me to my face that if I'm not gonna work here, I won't work anywhere. All of this was so mentally overwhelming because it's happening in real time, but you still have to show up and perform. Even though your colleagues know something isn't right here, but everyone's afraid to say something. You're being paid the same as everybody that's being promoted, but you're not being promoted. But you're being paid the same as them. There were a lot of different layers to the experience, which [...] I think one of the greatest things I was so proud of myself about was starting the DEIB [Diversity Equity Inclusion and Belonging] strategy and programme plan for the office, which then influenced the US to build out a wider plan, working with the senior leadership team, so the C-Suite team [were] on it.

I look back now and I think maybe they allowed me to do it to keep me quiet, but I think at the end of the experience where I think it was after one D&I [Diversity and Inclusion] training session, my manager called me and admitted after that session that she was aware because I was the only woman of colour in the office. It's like she had a moment where she realised that. And I'll never forget this. I always tell it [this story] verbatim that she allowed her personal pieces from her personal experiences into the workplace to impact my career projection and journey in the office because at that time I had just said to her that I'm going to leave. So that's a long winded answer but [...]

Interviewer. So basically she was holding back because of her own holding you back because of her own personal experiences and biases and was actually open about that.

Interviewee 8: Yeah, she admitted it when I had announced I was going to resign and it then made sense as to why [with] all the other senior directors that I would work with there would always be little issues, but then I'd ask teams what's actually going on [and] everyone's like "it's fine" and like we even used to test it [...]. So we had a client, really a retained (regular) client and what I'd do is I'd have my colleague who's one of my best friends now I'd have her submit the work to the coach. Yeah, and there'd be no issue. This is great, [name of colleague]. Oh, my God. You always deliver great work, blah blah. And then what I'd do is I'd submit [my colleague's] work to see if anyone would catch on to see—can you see the difference in the tone of voice? Even though we're writing for the client or the writing style? Or are you just so prepared to find an issue with me that it doesn't matter what it is you're always going to have an issue and lo and behold. You know, I'd said submit her work. "Oh, this is great, but this needs editing." This doesn't really align. This doesn't make sense. [They'd say] Ohh [name of colleague], could you have a look at it? And [colleague] would turn around and say what I actually drafted and worked with [interviewee 8] on this. I actually wrote this. Actually, we got to the point where we were like, we wrote it together. So what's the issue? So there were a lot of different things but [...] it's been a journey.

Questions for discussion:

1 How can organisations nurture diverse talent?
2 If you were a senior leader in this organisation and heard an employee give this account what would you do? For instance, who or what would you turn to for advice? What actions would you recommend the organisation adopt to encourage a more inclusive workplace?

Recruitment, Promotion and Everyday Life

Many, though not all, of the practitioners interviewed faced challenges in securing their first job or receiving what they considered fair promotion. While white, working-class practitioners often blamed these struggles to their own lack of confidence (as discussed later in the section on programmes aimed to increase diversity) their accent or their geographical location practitioners from ethnic minorities frequently explicitly or implicitly identified racism or bias as underlying causes. But in some areas of public relations and the media, racial diversity is notably absent as Interviewee 9 highlighted saying: "I've yet to work alongside a single ethnic minority person in PR." This lack of representation demonstrates that recruitment and promotion is not straightforward for those from a minority background, as further illustrated by Interviewee 2:

> I was being continually expected to work above my pay grade but they were never going to show any sign of actually rewarding me for that financially or remunerating me or giving me the title that I deserve to match the responsibility that, off the record, realistically that I had cause that you know it was never in my contract.

Many interviewees discussed how powerless they felt—they recognised that racism or systemic bias was present—, but since it existed at an organisational or cultural level rather than being attributed to individual actions, it was challenging to hold anyone accountable:

> It's so disheartening because I'm part of the People of Colours group in [city] where there's over 200 of us that have gone through certain things where, again, because there is no one holding anyone accountable and doing making the changes to say you know we're going to stamp out this kind of behaviour, we're going to take it seriously because we value you then.
>
> (Interviewee 8)

Even if overt discrimination was not always evident, the feeling of not belonging lingered:

> Even if nobody's treating you differently, you yourself feel like you don't belong. So how do you overcome that? [...] I'm not the kind of person to, as you might have guessed, be quiet and sit in the corner and not share my views so people know what my views are. But still to this day I always say to people who come from different backgrounds that you will still have to work harder than your white middle class ally colleagues and peers.
>
> (Interviewee 10)

This statement is amplified by findings of the UK Black Comms Network (2024) survey, which revealed that 67% of Black and Mixed Black professionals feel compelled to "tone down" their personalities at work, while 58% avoid social gatherings due to a sense of not fitting in with their colleagues. Given the communications industry's heavy reliance on informal networking for career advancement and recognition, it becomes evident how such experiences contribute to the underrepresentation of ethnic minorities practitioners in senior roles. In addition to these challenges, the age-related bias as a barrier to both recruitment and promotion—and the resulting lack of generational diversity in the sector—was raised by several participants. This bias was even more difficult to prove since whether someone is "too old" or "too young" is highly subjective. Interviewee 9 illustrated this challenge, sharing reflections on their personal experience:

> I do think age [is a factor] and sometimes I find it a bit frustrating because they [younger applicants] don't have the knowledge that I do or the experience and this was the particular case [when not being employed by a large public sector employer] and I don't think it was to do with my race.

Similarly, Interviewee 2 added:

> I think age is something which is probably played into [with] me being treated, perhaps a bit differently or not so fairly.

Reading 4 Extended Interview Extract: Working with Diverse Audiences and Producing Inclusive Communications. Interviewee 9 Discusses Their Experience

Interviewee 9: I did a contract [communications work] during 2021 for [large public sector organisation] and that was to do with the COVID vaccination campaign, where actually my background was very helpful because one of the key aims of the comms was to ensure that people from ethnic minority communities were getting vaccinated and there was a massive push nationally and there was a lot of like comms devoted [to it as] all the data had shown that there's a lot of vaccine hesitancy among minorities.

I worked on that which was quite successful, but interestingly enough as the year went on and it became clear from the data that in [northern regional town] anyway, the campaign to get people from ethnic minority backgrounds vaccinated was becoming successful [but] less so amongst working class communities. Now my feeling is that this was being replicated nationally. A lot of it was to do with conspiracy theories, but there was a lot of vaccine hesitancy.

So that was one area where [my background] was useful because obviously I've worked with these communities. I live in the community as well, but I was trying to convince [management] it wasn't just PR [we needed] engagement as well.

I did a short stint at [English regional local authority] and I remember that when I was prepping for the interview I went through their social media like you do just to see what they've been doing so that you know, if they ask you any questions that you [know what to talk about]. I'm glad I did because one of the questions was, "is there anything that we've done recently that you think we could have done better?" It was something along those lines. And I went, actually, yes, there is. I said I looked on your Twitter account and you were telling Muslim community not to break any social distancing rules for Eid, which is, you know, the Muslim festival and I said: "But you didn't actually wish them Eid Mubarak, you know, like you'd wish a happy Christmas." And she [the interviewer] went: "Yeah. And the members of the Muslim community have raised that with us."

Questions for discussion:

1 Do you think that it is the role of a practitioner from an ethnic minority background to ensure awareness of the cultural needs of an organisation's stakeholders?
2 What are the issues or concerns around using the culturally-specific expertise of a practitioner from a minority background?

Strand 2: Access and Impact of Initiatives Designed to Encourage Diversity in Public Relations

Research by Bourne (2022) and Edwards (2014a, 2023) acknowledged that while initiatives designed to increase diversity in public relations are well-intentioned, they often default to promoting white, middle-class behaviour as the "norm." In contrast, insights from interviews suggested a different perspective; graduates of such training programmes tend to not be aware of such issues or, if aware, emphasise the value that they have brought to their lives.

This divergence remarks a critical tension in the sector which is that the presence of diversity initiatives not always translate into meaningful career progression for underrepresented groups; as Interviewee 10 suggested:

> I think the challenge isn't the diversity […] it's the career progression that comes with it. Where are your leaders and why are we still in this? What feels like a diverse environment [is still] not able to produce senior level communicators and senior level professionals in other functions as well.

Therefore, while initiatives can provide valuable opportunities for minority groups, systemic barriers to career progression and leadership often remain unaddressed. To delve deeper into these dynamics, this strand examines the access to diversity initiatives and participants' experiences within these programmes, their impact on career development, and their influence on broader social mobility within the public relations profession.

Access to Initiatives and Experiences of Training Programmes

Access to initiatives and participation in diversity-focused programmes was frequently discussed by interviewees, many of whom shared positive experiences of programmes designed to encourage individuals from minority backgrounds in entering or advancing within the public relations industry. However, such training programmes often rely on established networks like LinkedIn, Twitter/X, industry bodies such as the Chartered Institute of Public Relations, and personal connections to publicise their opportunities. This can unintentionally limit the reach of the initiatives, excluding those who do not already occupy these business-focused online or social spaces, narrowing the pool of applicants.

While networks like BME PR Pros and the UK Black Comms Network help to widen the reach of such initiatives as well as running their own industry mentor programmes for Black, Asian and ethnic minority practitioners, the fact that many interviewees learned about programmes like the Taylor Bennett Foundation and Socially Mobile through LinkedIn, Twitter/X, and personal contact suggests giving such programmes a wider reach beyond established industry networks is an ongoing challenge which is difficult to fully resolve.

The motivations for applying for the programmes mentioned above varied, but were all largely linked to career advancement. The affordable or free nature of these programmes was a significant factor, alongside the fact that they were aimed to meet the needs of minority practitioners. As interviewee 5 noted:

> I wanted to do a management course but I couldn't afford to do it myself [...]. I was just looking around and I saw a post about it and I decided to apply for it, so yeah. And my work I don't want to put any staff through courses; they're not interested in career development. So I managed [...] just to do it myself.

Other participants highlighted the practical benefits they could gain from the training programmes:

> [I]t provided a really good understanding of media relations, social media, stakeholder engagement, media monitoring and analysis. It really brought a lot of awareness to the work that I was already doing as a former journalist and editor, and it was almost like that, missing link that I didn't know my career needed.
>
> (Interviewee 8)

> I was looking for, you know, a balance between the theory but practical skills to kind of leverage myself better in the workplace, as a comms professional.
>
> (Interviewee 2)

Additionally, the enthusiasm and positive feedback from previous cohorts also played a crucial role in applicants' decisions. As one participant shared:

> I had a chat with one of them, who was from one of the previous cohorts, and she was so enthusiastic about it.
>
> (Interviewee 2)

This personal endorsement from previous participants demonstrated the programme's potential to create tangible benefits, further motivating others.

Impact on Career

The role of diversity initiatives in shaping career trajectories emerged as a significant theme among participants. These training programmes were acknowledged for fostering personal growth, enhancing confidence, and opening doors to professional development opportunities.

The participants shared how training programmes impacted their careers within public relations, emphasising both the boost in confidence and the professional development opportunities. For Interviewee 6, the programme fostered self-belief:

> Confidence is one of the things that I've struggled with in my career, I think. And I think Socially Mobile has really helped me to have a bit more self-belief in some of the things that I actually do know and I'm good at and skills that I can offer.

Similarly, others credited that personal branding exercises made them reflect on their goals:

> [In the programme] you do personal branding quite early in the course and I've done a bit of life coaching as well at the same time, around about the same time someone was [being] trained and I was helping him. And the combination of the two things was pushing me to like, think about what I wanted in life.
>
> (Interviewee 7)

> I think it does make a difference because It's giving people like me more confidence to go out there and say, you know, I can do as I can be a manager in PR.
>
> (Interviewee 5)

While participants credited such programmes for shift in how they perceived career opportunities:

> I think the biggest thing has been just confidence in what I've got to offer, what my value is and It sounds really obvious, but just really thinking about my own CPD [Continuing Professional Development] and how I can build on that as well.
>
> (Interviewee 6)

This confidence also translated into the development of practical skills and skills learned:

> It's helped me as a person in terms of the skills and what I bring to my workplace.
>
> (Interviewee 2)

> I feel like it's just armed me with a bit of a toolkit that I can now use, you know, and it's helped me.
>
> (Interviewee 6)

Some participants also noted advancement into positions of responsibility after completing the programme:

> But what it [the scheme] does is give confidence to future leaders that are [from a] different background [...]—a diverse background. Someone like me [...]. It's probably a really good example [...] because most of us have gone on to change, like the majority of us have taken a senior post after doing it, [the fact] they're in power is pretty good.
>
> (Interviewee 22)

Reading 5 Career Trajectories and Leadership. Interviewee 10 Discusses his Experience

Interviewee 10: [When considering] the intersectionality between class and ethnically diverse backgrounds you [realise] don't necessarily have the connections [or] networks. So, you know, you'd hear "it's about who you know as much as what you know" and you'd dismiss it. And at that time, I dismissed it. It's not until you reflect back and realise how difficult it is to secure that first job in the industry and also like any other graduate, you think you can do any job in the world and you might not read every JD [job description] very carefully. But even the entry level roles, it was a real challenge.

For every reason, the right door took a while to open, and I truly believe that some of that's down to connections, and the ability to present yourself. You know, all my friends [...] might be in careers, but they live in working class areas. None of us have really moved far from where we originally lived. We went to the same school and we've kept in touch. So those are my networks and my networks were non-PR people or these people went through the university system with me [but] did accountancy, did law, did the other courses.

And it's a challenge now if you look at our [PR] profession, 92% are from non-ethnically diverse backgrounds. If your networks are limited [it's challenging to get a role in PR]. You probably didn't invest much time [in building networks] because you weren't taught that at school. So when you're coming through the schools, I think it's a challenging environment where [your education was at] a city comprehensive [state-controlled non-selective school for children from the local area].

Well, I think the teachers have got the challenge of making sure you behave yourself first and foremost and, you know, hopefully getting [you] just the minimum results. Whereas in other schools you're probably pushed hard and then you've got a supportive home network—my family was very supportive just to be really clear. But your wider network was probably more interested in encouraging you to go out and play football and do other things that young people do.

So all that contributes to the challenges you have in terms of securing your first role and then progressing. And it took me probably [until] joining the [large public sector organisation] to realise [that] some of the barriers you have because I never talk about, I never talked about race and racism because I thought that was people shoving shit through your letterbox because that's what my dad and his generation had to put with it and I didn't see any of that. I'd say: "I don't know what you're on about. There's no such thing as racism." And it's only then when you hear the actual experience of others and you understand and reflect and think [that] actually there were probably opportunities [where it] could easily have [happened] and [it was the reason why] I didn't get the role I should have got and I wasn't afforded the opportunities I should have been afforded.

[...]

[My current organisation is] very diverse. You'd hope so with [so many] employees, but in the comms profession, there's work to do. In terms of diversity, where have we got [to]? A diverse group of colleagues in comms, most of them are in junior/middle management roles.But where are you more senior communicators? Sometimes I'm embarrassed when I look around in the north of England and see myself as one of the most senior communicators from an ethnically diverse background in [my organisation]. So I think the challenge isn't the diversity [...] It's the career progression that comes with it. Where are your leaders and why are we still like this? What feels like a diverse environment is not able to produce senior level communicators and senior level professionals in other functions as well.

Interviewer: Why do you think there's an issue with retention and promotion to the senior grades?

Interviewee 10: There's probably multiple reasons some of it could be bias, conscious or otherwise, and discrimination whichever way you want to describe it. I think sometimes it's about people not being offered the same opportunities. [For instance] where's the training and development opportunities? Who's getting them? Who's having to work harder to prove themselves, whose mistakes are magnified more than others? Who is challenging and disrupting the way we do communications so that we listen to their views of our diverse teams, including those, for example, with neurodivergent health issues? They bring a level of creativity that you're not going to get from others potentially. So I think there's a number of challenges and look, people in power will always be concerned about those who want to then be part of that power dynamic and new power comes with a sense of intrigue and nervousness. So there's multiple barriers. And then sometimes I think—are the right mentors in place? Have you got the right coaches? Are people paying it forward often enough? So there's multiple challenges, but it's for people like me and allies to think about what we do to overcome some of the challenges we face, even if at the time, like I said, I didn't recognise it, but others recognised it straight away. So [there are] hurdles have you overcome and how can you help others?

And then a couple of years ago [we wanted to recruit someone]. And because we went through [a recruitment agency], there was a relatively young Asian male who I thought if it was the normal standard application process, you wouldn't get through, but the level we're looking at—[I thought] what can you offer? Well come and give it a shot and between as will help you out. So then it's that coaching in a work setting, because I think that's the other challenge that people have that don't know how to conduct themselves in different settings. So when you're progressing through the ranks, how you behave in a boardroom is different to how you might behave in a team meeting setting. Again, who's supporting people in that space so that they become a brand in themselves and be developed.

[...]

Even if nobody's treating you differently, you yourself feel like you don't belong. So how do you overcome that? I always say to people who come from different backgrounds that you will still have to work harder than your white middle class ally colleagues and peers. You will always have to cover yourself, cover your back more I feel than you would if you were from a different background?

I would say the challenge is when you're in that environment and you're either a disruptor or innovator or you're disruptive and destructive. So it depends how people see it.

Questions for discussion:

1 How many barriers can you identify to (i) getting your first role in PR and (ii) getting promoted once in a PR role
2 How can organisations recognise and recruit people who come from diverse backgrounds. What needs to change?

Impact on Social Mobility

Whether the training programmes discussed do or do not propagate a white middle class way of working was not something of concern to our interviewees. What the interviews showed was that training programmes designed to increase diversity potentially did three things. Firstly, they respected the differences that the participants brought to the training programme with Interviewee 13 noting that "they [such training programmes] do us justice and secondly, the scheme gave them confidence in their abilities." Potentially, this means that the interviewees were able to bring their particular style of working, related to their diversity, into the workplace. Secondly, they gave interviewees confidence and thirdly, the training programmes gave participants knowledge, although this was mentioned less often.

Confidence in abilities can be seen as intangible, but to participants it was often what they lacked to move forward in their career. Writing on confidence or self-confidence from a variety of perspectives links it (or lack of it) to gender (e.g., Lenney, 1977), social class (e.g., Croizet & Claire, 1998) and race (e.g., Litzler et al., 2014). However, little has been written about self-confidence among public relations practitioners, and while Wigley and Zhang (2014) related confidence in a public relations setting to preparedness and planning, the interviewees saw it in a wider context:

Confidence is [...] one of the things that I've struggled with in my career, I think. And I think [training programme] has really helped me to have a

> bit more self-belief in some of the things that I actually do know and I'm good at and skills that I can offer.
>
> (Interviewee 6)

> [The training programme was good for] just sharpening a lot of skills, lots of new stuff, you know, so the sort of reassurance factor that actually maybe I wasn't a million miles off in the first place [in terms of what] I've been doing. And just [to] have that reassurance that some of the stuff is best practice that I'm, you know, I'm doing and the key things really [are the] strategic side and so planning, evaluation, leadership, and managing teams, things like that, skills where I felt because I don't have a team of my own at the moment at work.
>
> (Interviewee 1)

The interviews uncovered a paradox in that many felt that the course helped them to fit in—but on the course's terms. Some, however, felt the programmes put them in a better place-but one where there was still discrimination.

> Whether it's one piece of new information you get or it's a new opportunity, you get a new job opportunity. You're able to [...] build relationships with people in the industry, you would have never met via the [scheme] or because of the [training programme].
>
> (Interviewee 8)

For others, the networks formed afterwards were as valuable as the course itself:

> So there's a whole network of my cohort that we've all kind of kept in touch with each other or kind of championing [supporting/advocating for] each other, and the wider cohort as well. So it's really brilliant.
>
> (Interviewee 6)

Conclusion

In this chapter, we examined how initiatives designed to promote diversity in the public relations industry impact the professional career of Black, Asian and ethnic minority practitioners. The conversations with participants also collected insights from their experiences in training programmes designed to increase their presence in public relations. The impact of these programmes included increased confidence, the development of key skills, and the creation of professional networks, providing valuable opportunities in a historically homogenous environment.

However, despite progress in terms of the number of initiatives and reports, structural barriers in terms of race, discrimination and lack of representation in leadership positions in the public relations industry remain significant obstacles with the number of Black, Asian, ethnic minority and working class practitioners potentially decreasing in number. While these initiatives open doors to new opportunities, the key question is how to ensure that this access translates into lasting change in career paths and equitable progression.

It is crucial to continue to reflect on how to transform these initiatives to ensure that they not only provide entry opportunities, but also facilitate true diversity and mobility within the profession. This change, however, may lie in the leadership of the public relations profession itself and more realistically, into society beyond that, before real change is visible.

3 Current Challenges and Pathways to a Truly Diverse Future

When we proposed and wrote this book, the public relations industry was going through an ongoing period of change in how race, diversity, identity, and social mobility were perceived and debated. While these issues have gained visibility and become increasingly integrated into everyday discussions and actions, a range of reports including those by the Black Comms Network (2024), NHS Communicate (2024), PRCA Race and Ethnicity Equity Board (2024) and the Chartered Institute of Public Relations (2024) suggests that the many initiatives mentioned in Chapters One and Two have had limited impact, failing to address deep-seated structural inequalities.

Today, conversations around diversity in the public relations industry are evolving beyond academic and activist debates with increasing attention on the intersections of race with other diversity dimensions (such as social class, disability, and age), and the need for social mobility in the practice. Yet, this increasing awareness and recognition of diversity—at least among practitioners on social channels and in industry magazines and on conference stages—must be considered within the wider political and social changes. In 2024, various general elections worldwide have resulted in a range of political outcomes, with governments prioritising issues like immigration policies and social rights that influence the broader landscape for equality and diversity. Among this, many conservative or consolidated autocratic governments have employed exclusionary rhetoric or actively eroded rights, particularly those of women and marginalised communities (Carothers, 2024). These changes underscore the complex and evolving dynamics in addressing diversity within the public relations profession.

In the UK, for example, the Chartered Institute of Public Relations' *State of the Profession* survey revealed the ongoing challenges related to the retention and career progression of diverse professionals from diverse backgrounds (Chartered Institute of Public Relations, 2024). Furthermore, the economic environment, such as the cost of living crisis, has impacted diversity training programmes, potentially making them more difficult to sustain financially. In November 2024, Socially Mobile (whose graduates were among our

DOI: 10.4324/9781032692234-4

interviewees) made an appeal for funding in order to continue operations into 2025 (Waddington, 2024).

In light of this context recent research, including those from Munshi and Kurian (2022) and Gregory (2020), provided interesting reflections about challenges of the public relations industry in light of social and technological changes as well as allowing us to explore some of the thinking around the lack of diversity in the occupation. As we have seen, the Chartered Institute of Public Relations report (2022) has observed that the public relations industry is still largely dominated by white, middle-class and privately educated practitioners and Gregory (2020) has criticised the profession for its exclusivity, stating that it "does not open its doors, make welcome, reward or honour its own diverse community" (p. 401). Expanding on this point, Gregory highlighted:

> The profession has been highly successful in maintaining barriers to entry and progression: the more traditional social elites—typically white, middle-class, and well-educated still dominate. What is needed now is more positive action to break these barriers or the profession not only risks becoming its own stereotype, but it limits its ability to fulfil its potential as well. In terms of social closure, public relations is still treated with suspicion and is unable to shake off its dubious image.
>
> (Gregory, 2022, p. 403)

This action is much needed. Research by the industry body Black Comms Network (2024) found that "two-thirds (67%) of Black and Mixed-Black communications professionals surveyed reported that, as new hires, they felt the need to 'tone down' their personalities to fit into the workplace environment" (p. 15), and that there may have been a regression in progress over the last four years.

Meanwhile, Munshi and Kurian (2022) advocated for a more radical approach. They proposed the idea of "insurgent" public relations—a transformative shift in the profession's power structures that could allow for a more diverse future. These ideas resonate with movements that seek to bring together historically marginalised groups in the pursuit of justice, equity, and diversity:

> A system change needs a radically different narrative of resistance to take shape, a narrative disseminated through an insurgent public relations. In some of our own work, we have documented what we call "movements of determined resistance" (Bhavnani et al., 2016). These movements often create networks of groups and are frequently fronted by women in conjunction with Indigenous communities and other historically marginalized publics working towards a "future that is inclusive, diverse, just, equitable and democratic, one that is based on a recognition of the dignity of all

> lives, human and non-human" (Bhavnani et al., 2016, p. xxii). Meanwhile, in the public relations discipline itself, new networks of theorizing have emerged which explore how public relations is implicated in creating and maintaining dominant social and cultural hierarchies and inequalities.
>
> (Munshi & Kurian, 2022, p. 403)

At the same time, there are critiques of some diversity initiatives. Bananuka (2024) from the campaigning group BME PR Pros highlighted the problems with tokenistic approaches, which she says often do more harm than good. She emphasised the importance of embedding diverse voices in leadership roles within diversity programmes and pointed out some of the issues inherent in recruitment practices that fail to attract and retain a diverse workforce. As she reports on the BME PR Pros website:

> I think that there are some pretty crappy initiatives out there that do more harm than good. That a lot of work is tokenistic. That the Diversity and Inclusion (D&I) sector and consultants can be part of the problem. That recruitment consultants are part of the problem. That BMEs should be front and centre of BME diversity initiatives. That diversity in PR and comms isn't a BME problem but a sector problem. I don't believe only people with white skin can write press releases, create creative campaigns, lead teams, run businesses etc. etc. If you don't get BMEs applying for your jobs, then there's a problem in your recruitment practices. If you have a BME retention problem, then there's something wrong with your working culture.
>
> (par. 26)

Despite or because of these reservations—some voiced by the founders of similar organisations which aim to increase diversity in public relations—there has been a significant rise in the number and scale of initiatives aimed at supporting practitioners from diverse backgrounds. Notably, examples include:

- Awards ceremonies such as the PROs Awards theprosawards.com. These annual awards were founded in the UK in 2023 and celebrate talented UK-based Black, Asian, mixed race and ethnic minority public relations and communications professionals and agencies owned and founded by them. The awards also aim to celebrate public relations and communications work targeting Black, Asian, mixed race and ethnic minority consumers.
- The creation of organisations aiming to champion and support women in the workplace during specific life stages such as PR Mums; as well as organisations to support ethnic minority professionals to access leadership roles both inside and outside public relations through programmes such as Board Apprentice.

- The growth of networks aimed at Black, Asian and ethnic minority public relations practitioners such as The Xec, Black Comms Network, BME PR Pros and the Asian Communications Network. These networks offer mentorship, visibility and industry connections.
- Conferences such as Make Comms Great Again—a 2024 conference for public relations and communications professionals with a speaker panel where speakers from Black, Asian, mixed race and ethnic minority backgrounds were in the majority.

Reading 6 Further Reading: Organisations at the Forefront of Promoting the Benefits of Diversity and Supporting and Campaigning for Diversity in Public Relations (URLs correct at the time of publication)

This list is largely UK-focussed and relates mostly to organisations working in the area of public relations and communications. However, many similar organisations exist in different sectors and countries/regions.

Awards

PROs Awards theprosawards.com

Campaigning and Support Organisations

Asian Communications Network https://www.linkedin.com/company/asian-communications-network/
BME PR Pros https://bmeprpros.co.uk/
Chartered Institute of Public Relations Diversity and Inclusion Network https://www.cipr.co.uk/CIPR/Network/Groups_/Diversity_and_Inclusion_Network.aspx
Inclusive Public Relations https://inpr.uk/
PR Mums https://www.pr-mums.com
UK Black Comms Network https://inpr.uk/
Women in PR https://womeninpr.org.uk/

Training, Coaching and Accreditation

Board Apprentice https://www.boardapprentice.com/
The Blueprint https://bmeprpros.co.uk/blueprint/
The Xec https://bmeprpros.co.uk/the-xec/

Socially Mobile https://www.sociallymobile.org.uk/
Taylor Bennett Foundation https://www.taylorbennettfoundation.org/

Reports, Guides, and Resources

Accessible Communications: Resources from the Chartered Institute of Public Relations
https://cipr.co.uk/CIPR/CIPR/Our_work/Policy/Accessible_Communications.aspx
Race in PR: BAME lived experiences in the PR industry https://cipr.co.uk/CIPR/Our_work/Policy/Diversity_resources.aspx
Disability Equality at Work: Resources from the Chartered Institute of Personnel and Development Disability at work | CIPD https://www.cipd.org/uk/views-and-insights/cipd-viewpoint/disability-work/
Disability allyship and advocacy: A guide from the Chartered Institute of Public Relations' Diversity and Inclusion Network https://cipr.co.uk/common/Uploaded%20files/About%20us/CIPR_Diversity_Inclusion_Disabilty_Allyship_and_Advocacy.pdf
From Words to Change. Four Years On: Ethnicity pay gap reporting in the communications sector https://www.flipsnack.com/prcauk/from-words-to-change/full-view.html
Global Women in PR Annual Index https://globalwpr.com/annual-index/
One step forward two steps black: Report from Black Comms Network https://static1.squarespace.com/static/5eeb1c625cddf3179c2d330d/t/66ad2c2ad913620d936ac4a1/1722625081718/BCN_Report_2024_FINAL.pdf
Understanding accessibility requirements for public sector bodies: information and resources from the UK government
Understanding accessibility requirements for public sector bodies—GOV.UK

In addition, we have seen more discussion and understanding of intersectionality (which was referred to at the start of Chapter 1). Intersectionality, as we explained, is more than just having multiple identities; it is a framework that reveals how specific groups face unique challenges when multiple identities overlap in a system that may not have been designed for them. Cho et al. (2013) discussed how this theory threw a spotlight on people with intersecting identities (race, gender, class, disability) often experiencing discrimination that can't be fully understood by looking at each identity on its own.

We cannot discuss the current and future challenges relating to diversity in public relations without considering the role of developments in artificial intelligence (AI). AI systems have been criticised for their bias; for instance there have been various reports looking at racial, sexual and age-related bias in AI facial recognition systems and a study by Bogen and Rieke (2018) found that AI-supported recruiting displayed anti-Black bias in part due to a lack of diversity among engineers who develop AI. However, a report by consultants

Korn Ferry (n.d.) observed opportunities for practitioners to work with AI to reduce bias and increase inclusivity. This included:

- For AI to listen to the audio of meetings to see who is dominating the conversation, and who is being overlooked (although the report adds that the onus is on employees to change behaviour).
- Using AI to look across the workforce and identify talent that may not otherwise apply or be considered for promotion. This can help diversify a firm's upper ranks better than humans, who might tend to select individuals for certain roles from within their personal networks—which is often reflective of only one demographic.

While the body of literature on AI and diversity is growing, scholarship which reflects the challenges and opportunities that AI brings to public relations (e.g., Chartered Institute of Public Relations, 2023; Gregory, 2023) tends not to put a central focus on diversity, pointing to a valid future research area.

Although writers such as Chi et al. (2021) reported a mixed picture when discussing the intersection of ethics, AI, and diversity they do note that there are now an increasing number of tools and publications aimed at engineering diverse, fair, and inclusive products and services. They observed that:

> [I]n the absence of a diverse workforce, firms can still push forward diversity and inclusion goals in the form of diverse data sets or personalization tools that can accommodate diverse behaviors and contexts. While these latter goals and work flows may produce better customer experiences, changing data practices may very well be easier than altering hiring practices, corporate culture, and business models, which are all easier than addressing the structural inequalities that civil rights laws seek to address. (p. 10)

Global efforts to raise awareness and effect change must expand, particularly at a macro level (government policies and large-scale industry changes), meso level (organisational diversity programs and community outreach), and micro level (individual actions within workplaces). These actions should be intertwined to create a cohesive global movement that encourages more diverse voices and contributes to systemic change.

At the macro level, governments and international bodies must implement policies that promote diversity in all industries, including public relations. Public relations firms should be incentivised to build more inclusive cultures, not only through recruitment but by revising organisational structures and technology that might inadvertently marginalise practitioners from diverse backgrounds.

On the meso level, large-scale industry bodies need to increase their efforts in fostering diversity. This could be by expanding networking opportunities, creating mentoring programmes, and supporting initiatives that offer leadership opportunities for practitioners from diverse backgrounds not only in the UK, but also around the world. Internationally, networks like the UK Black Comms Network or the Asian Communications Network could work together to establish global partnerships, sharing best practices and amplifying their impact across borders.

At the micro level, individual practitioners must recognise their role in challenging biases, fostering inclusivity, and advocating for their colleagues. While initiatives at larger scales are vital, the true transformation of the industry will depend on the commitment of every professional to the cause. Whether by speaking out against discrimination, creating campaigns that recognise the diversity of modern audiences, or mentoring young professionals, each practitioner can contribute to the evolving narrative of diversity in the field.

To this, it is essential to consider the role of education in driving long-term change. According to Bardhan and Gower (2020), educators have a critical responsibility to shape the future of the profession by ensuring that future professionals are not only aware of the challenges faced by underrepresented groups but are also equipped with the necessary skills to implement practices of diversity. Furthermore, these students, when they become leaders and managers in the future, will act in line with their awareness. If they recognise the importance of diversity and equity, they are more likely to lead by example, creating diverse teams and organisational cultures that promote long-term, sustainable change.

As discussed throughout this book, the public relations industry is taking action to make the field more diverse—both in terms of its stakeholders and its practitioners. The *State of NHS Communications* report (NHS Communicate, 2024), which noted the historically low number of ethnic minorities in senior roles within the UK National Health Service, emphasised the need for change. The report calls for the creation of a task force to address the root causes of this issue:

> [This] report calls for the creation of a taskforce to explore the root causes of why so few of the most senior NHS communicators are from an ethnic minority background, and to make recommendations for how a more ethnically diverse leadership can be achieved. This taskforce should consist of communications leaders from local NHS organisations; NHS Providers, NHS Confederation, NHS England and other national bodies; and experts in the field of diversity and inclusion who can provide guidance on how other sectors have tackled this issue.
>
> (p. 21)

Meanwhile, the UK Black Comms Network report (2024) took a more direct approach, offering clear guidance on the issue:

> We need to start speaking to white colleagues about their behaviour and their actions. We keep speaking to the oppressed about what they can do

> to change or avoid and it's not fixing the problem at hand. We have an un-diverse, uncomfortable industry until those with the bad behaviour—the unconscious bias changes.
>
> (Black Comms Network, 2024, p. 30)

The report outlined several interventions believed by those surveyed to be effective in improving representation. These interventions included:

- Industry specific initiatives such as the UK Black Comms Network (77%)
- Increased diversity across board members (76%)
- Invitations to senior level events (69%).
- Networking events (66%)
- Mentoring (68%)

Meanwhile, the PRCA *Race and Ethnicity Equity Board* report (2024) called for a targeted approach at a junior level to reduce pay gaps based on ethnicity and to improve future representation at senior levels. It noted the importance of conducting regular pay gap analysis and monitoring the process of ethnic minority practitioners.

The ongoing discussions and reports referenced throughout this book highlight the complexity and urgency of transforming the public relations field into a more diverse and equity space. As this chapter—and indeed this entire book—demonstrates there is no single course of action that can make the public relations occupation more diverse. The solutions that work for one person, group, or organisation may not be applicable to others, underscoring the need for a more tailored approach. In addition, against the backdrop of an unequal and possibly fractured society where institutional bias is entrenched, the task may seem monumental.

However, that is no reason for apathy or inaction. On the contrary, as evidenced by both the individual and collective efforts discussed here, each step taken—no matter how small—can contribute to meaningful change. From policy adjustments to the advocacy for diversity, these actions demonstrate that improvement is achievable. Ultimately, the responsibility lies not only with the organisations and institutions but also with each individual practitioner. By fostering an environment where equity and diversity are championed, we can help to build a public relations industry that is representative, fair, and truly reflective of the diverse society it serves.

Bibliography

Abdullah, Z. (2007). Towards international cultural diversity management of public relations: Viewpoints of chairmen/CEOs. *International Journal of Economics Management*, *1*(2), 285–299. https://psasir.upm.edu.my/id/eprint/722/1/bab06.pdf

Ahmed, S. (2012). *On being included: Racism and diversity in institutional life*. Duke University Press.

Al-Jenaibi, B. (2011). Gender issues in the diversity and practice of public relations in the UAE case study of PR male managers and female PR practitioners. *International Journal of E-Politics*, *2*(3), 35–56. https://doi.org/10.4018/jep.2011070104

Anderson, R. C. (2006). Teaching (with) disability: Pedagogies of lived experience. *The Review of Education, Pedagogy, and Cultural Studies*, *28*(3–4), 367–379. https://doi.org/10.1080/10714410600873258

Anthias, F. (2001). The concept of 'social division' and theorising social stratification: Looking at ethnicity and class. *Sociology, 35*(4), 835–854. https://www.jstor.org/stable/42856344

Anthias, F. (2013). Hierarchies of social location, class and intersectionality: Towards a translocational frame. *International Sociology, 28*(1), 121–138. https://doi.org/10.1177/0268580912463155

Applebaum, L. (2009, December 23). *Multiculturalism, diversity and PRSA: Trying something new*. Retrieved March 19, 2010 from: https://prsay.prsa.org/index.php/2009/12/23/multiculturalism-diversity-and-prsa-trying-something-new/

Ashby-King, D., & Anderson, L. (2023). Ventriloquizing institutional ethos: Social issues man-agement, internal public relations, and the institutionalization of neoliberalism and whiteness in U.S. universities' diversity discourse. *Journal of Public Relations Research*, *35*(5–6), 375–392. https://doi.org/10.1080/1062726X.2023.2198238

Austin, J. E. (2010). *The collaboration challenge: How nonprofits and businesses succeed through strategic alliances*. John Wiley & Sons.

Austin, L., Gaither, B., & Gaither, K. (2019). Corporate social advocacy as public interest communications: exploring perceptions of corporate involvement in controversial social-political issues. *The Journal of Public Interest Communications, 3*(2), 3. https://doi.org/10.32473/jpic.v3.i2.p3

Baird, S., & Bridgen, E. (2023). *Levelling up the public relations profession: A report sponsored by the Chartered Institute of Public Relations Research Fund*. CIPR. Retrieved from: https://www.slideshare.net/CIPRPaul/levelling-up-public-relations

Bananuka, E. (2024, January). Want to know more about BME PR Pros? No problem, here are answers to common questions. *BME PR Pros*. Retrieved from: https://bmeprpros.co.uk/faqs/

Banerjee, D. (2013). Workplace identities of women in the US labor market. *Sociology Mind, 3*, 19–24. https://doi.org/10.4236/sm.2013.31004

Bardhan, N., & Gower, K. (2020). Student and faculty/educator views on diversity and inclusion in public relations: The role of leaders in bringing about change. *Journal of Public Relations Education*, *6*(2), 102–141. https://journalofpreducation.com/wp-content/uploads/2022/12/d7c44-pdf-of-bardhan-and-gower-2020-from-jpre-6.2-1.pdf

Barrett, E. (2024). Agency leaders should encourage frank, honest discussions. *PR Week.* Retrieved from: https://www.prweek.com/article/1883273/agency-leaders-encourage-frank-honest-discussions-%E2%80%93-pr-reacts-uk-riots

Bassil, S. (2024, May 3). Supporting invisible conditions and disabilities in the PR workplace. *Influence.* Retrieved from: https://influenceonline.co.uk/2024/05/03/supporting-disabilities-invisible-conditions-in-the-PR-workplace

Bell, A. (2024). Beyond buzzwords. Embedding a systemic approach to EDI across the UK's professions. *Chartered Institute of Public Relations.* Retrieved from: cipr.co.uk/common/Uploaded files/Policy/Diversity/Full report - Beyond buzzwords.pdf

Benfield, T. (2019). What strategies can be implemented to best meet the needs of an ageing workforce?. flexible learning 4: Change Strategies, 31.

Bilge, S. (2010). Recent feminist outlooks on intersectionality. Diogenes, 57(1), 58–72.

Bilge, S., & Denis, A. (2010). Introduction: Women, intersectionality and diasporas. *Journal of Intercultural Studies, 31*(1), 1–8. https://doi.org/10.1080/07256860903487653

Bilge, N., Marino, M. I., & Webb, L. M. (2021). Definitions of ethnicity in communication scholarship: A new perspective. *Howard Journal of Communications, 32*(3), 213–234. https://doi.org/10.1080/10646175.2021.1871869

Bogen, M., & Rieke, A. (2018). Help wanted: An examination of hiring algorithms, equity, and bias. *Upturn,* December 7. Retrieved from: https://www.upturn.org/static/reports/2018/hiring-algorithms/files/Upturn%20--%20Help%20Wanted%20-%20An%20Exploration%20of%20Hiring%20Algorithms,%20Equity%20and%20Bias.pdf

Botan, C. H., & Sommerfeldt, E. (2023). Public relations theory III. Lawrence Erlbaum Associates.

Bourne, C. (2022). Public relations and the digital. London, UK, University of London. Be included. In *Public relations and the digital. Communicating in professions and organizations* (pp. 109–136). Palgrave Macmillan. https://doi.org/10.1007/978-3-031-13956-7_5

Bridgen, E (2018). Impact of diversity initiatives on practitioners and practice. In S. Waddington (Ed.), *Chartered institute of public relations 'Platinum' 70th anniversary* book pp. 219–223.

Bridgen, E. (2024). Just like any other: Public relations careers in the adult industry. In E. Bridgen and S. Williams (Eds.), *Women's work in public relations.* Emerald Publishing.

Brook O, O'Brien D, Taylor M (2018) There was no golden age: Social mobility into cultural and creative occupations. SocArXiv. Available at: https://osf.io/preprints/socarxiv/7njy3/

Bryman, A. (2016). *Social research methods*. Oxford University Press.

Cabosky, J. M. (2014). Framing an LGBT organization and a movement: A critical qualitative analysis of GLAAD'S media releases. Public Relations Inquiry, 3(1), 69–89

Carbado, D. W. (2013). Colorblind intersectionality. *Signs: Journal of Women in Culture and Society*, *38*(4), 811–845. https://doi.org/10.1086/669666

Carothers, T. (2024, September 3). How global democracy is faring in the year of elections. *Emissary*. Retrieved from: https://carnegieendowment.org/emissary/2024/08/elections-2024-democracy-autocracy-assessment?lang=en

Chartered Institute of Public Relations. (2020). *Race in PR: BAME lived experiences in the PR industry*. Chartered Institute of Public Relations. Retrieved from: https://cipr.co.uk/CIPR/Our_work/Policy/Diversity_resources.aspx

Chartered Institute of Public Relations. (2022a). *PR population report*. Chartered Institute of Public Relations. Retrieved from: https://cipr.co.uk/common/Uploaded%20files/Our%20work/POLICY/CIPR_PR_Population_Report%20(1).pdf

Chartered Institute of Public Relations. (2022b). *State of the profession report 2021/2022*. Chartered Institute of Public Relations. Retrieved from: https://www.cipr.co.uk/CIPR/Our_work/Policy/PR_research.aspx?WebsiteKey=0379ffac-bc76-433c-9a94-56a04331bf64

Chartered Institute of Public Relations. (2023). *AI tools and the impact on public relations*. Chartered Institute of Public Relations. Retrieved from: https://cipr.co.uk/CIPR/CIPR/Learn_Develop/Resources/AI_tools_and_the_impact_on_public_relations.aspx

Chartered Institute of Public Relations. (2024). *State of the profession report 2024*. Chartered Institute of Public Relations. Retrieved from: https://cipr.co.uk/common/Uploaded%20files/Policy/State%20of%20Prof/CIPR_State_of_the_Profession_2024.pdf

Chi, N., Lurie, E., & Mulligan, D. K. (2021). Reconfiguring diversity and inclusion for AI ethics. In *Proceedings of the 2021 AAAI/ACM conference on AI, ethics, and society* (pp. 447–457). https://doi.org/10.48550/arXiv.2105.02407

Childers Hon, L., & Brunner, B. (2000). Diversity issues and public relations. *Journal of Public Relations Research, 12*(4), 309–340. https://doi.org/10.1207/S1532754XJPRR1204_2

Cho, S., Crenshaw, K. W., & McCall, L. (2013). Toward a field of intersectionality studies: Theory, applications, and praxis. *Signs: Journal of Women in Culture and Society*, *38*(4), 785–810. https://doi.org/10.1086/669608

Ciszek, E. (2018). Queering PR: Directions in theory and research for public relations scholarship. *Journal of Public Relations Research*, *30*(4), 134–145. https://doi.org/10.1080/1062726X.2018.1440354

Ciszek, E., & Logan, N. (2018). Challenging the dialogic promise: How Ben & Jerry's support for black lives matter fosters dissensus on social media. *Journal of Public Relations Research 30*(3), 115–127. https://doi.org/10.1080/1062726X.2018.1498342

Cohen, N.S. (2015) Cultural work as a site of struggle. In Fuchs, C. & Mosco, V. (Eds.). (2016). Marx and the Political Economy of the Media (Vol. 79). Leiden: Brill.

Creative Industries Policy and Evidence Centre. (2021). *Social mobility in the creative economy: Rebuilding and levelling up?* Retrieved from: https://pec.ac.uk/research-reports/social-mobility-in-the-creative-economy-rebuilding-and-levelling-up

Croizet, J. C., & Claire, T. (1998). Extending the concept of stereotype threat to social class: The intellectual underperformance of students from low socioeconomic backgrounds. *Personality and Social Psychology Bulletin*, *24*(6), 588–594. https://doi.org/10.1177/0146167298246003

Cumberbatch, G., & Negrine, R. (2022). *Images of disability on television*. Routledge.

de Haan, D., Osborne, A., & Sherry, E. (2015). Satire or send-up? Paddy power and blind football: A case for managing public relations for disability sport. *Communication & Sport*, *3*(4), 411–433. https://doi.org/10.1177/2167479513518045

Delgado, R. (1989). Legal storytelling: Storytelling for oppositionists and others: A plea for narrative. Michigan Law Review, 87, 2411.

Delgado, R. and Stefancic, J. (2023) Introduction In Delgado, R. and Stefancic, J. (2023) *Critical race theory, fourth edition: An introduction* (pp1–2) NYU Press

Dello Russo, S., Antino, M., Zaniboni, S., Caetano, A., & Truxillo, D. (2021). The effect of age on daily positive emotions and work behaviors. *Work, Aging and Retirement*, *7*(1), 9–19. https://doi.org/10.1093/workar/waz026

Dhunna, A. (2019). The rama-dos and rama-don'ts of understanding Muslimes. *PR Week*. Retrieved from: https://www.prweek.com/article/1586812/rama-dos-rama-donts-understanding-muslims

Diggs-Brown, B., & Zaharna, R. S. (1995). Ethnic diversity in the public relations industry. *The Howard Journal of Communication, 6(*1–2), 114–123. https://doi.org/10.1080/10646179509361688

Eddo-Lodge, R. (2020). *Why I'm no longer talking to white people about race*. Bloomsbury.

Edwards, L. (2013). Institutional racism in cultural production: The case of public relations. *Popular Communication*, *11*(3), 242–256. https://doi.org/10.1080/15405702.2013.810084

Edwards, L. (2014a). *Power, diversity and public relations*. Routledge.

Edwards, L. (2014b). Discourse, credentialism and occupational closure in the communications industries: The case of public relations in the UK. *European Journal of Communication, 29*(3), 319–334. https://doi.org/10.1177/0267323113519228

Edwards, L. (2023). 'I'm a PR person. Let's just deal with it.' Managing intersectionality in professional life. *Public Relations Inquiry*, *12*(1), 27–51. https://doi.org/10.1177/2046147X221089323

Edwards, L., & Aulakh, S. (2024). Public relations recruitment as boundary-making: The client, the 'fit' and the disposability of diversity. *Public Relations Inquiry*, *13*(1), 93–112. https://doi.org/10.1177/2046147X231210277

Ertem-Eray, T., & Ki, E. J. (2021). The status of diversity research in public relations: An analysis of published articles. *PRism*, *17*(1), 1–21. https://www.prismjournal.org/uploads/1/2/5/6/125661607/final_published_word_document_tugce_prism.pdf

Fine, C., Sojo, V., & Lawford-Smith, H. (2020). Why does workplace gender diversity matter? Justice, organizational benefits, and policy. *Social Issues and Policy Review*, *14*(1), 36–72. https://doi.org/10.1111/sipr.12064

Fitch, K., & Third, A. (2010). Working girls: Revisiting the gendering of public relations. *PRism, 7*(4), 1–13. https://www.prismjournal.org/uploads/1/2/5/6/125661607/v7-no4-a1.pdf

Flegg, M. (2022). Why public relations must address its ageism problem. *Influence*. Retrieved from: https://influenceonline.co.uk/2022/02/04/why-public-relations-must-address-its-ageism-problem/

Fraga, L. R., Martinez-Ebers, V., Lopez, L., & Ricardo, R. (2005). *Strategic intersectionality: Gender, ethnicity, and political incorporation*. Presented at the 2005 Annual Meeting of the American Political Science Association, Washington, DC.

Fröhlich, R., & Peters, S. B. (2007). PR bunnies caught in the agency ghetto? Gender stereotypes, organizational factors, and women's careers in PR agencies. *Journal of Public Relations Research, 19*(3), 229–254. https://doi.org/10.1080/10627260701331754

Goethals, T., Mortelmans, D., Van den Bulck, H., Van den Heurck, W., & Van Hove, G. (2022). I am not your metaphor: Frames and counter-frames in the representation of disability. *Disability & Society*, *37*(5), 746–764. https://doi.org/10.1080/09687599.2020.1836478

Gregory, A. (2020). Chartered status and public relations' struggle for legitimacy. *Corporate Communications: An International Journal, 25*(4), 639–653. https://doi.org/10.1108/ccij-11-2019-0130

Gregory, A. (2022). Public relations practice equipped for the future: evolution or radical change?. In The Routledge Companion to Public Relations (pp. 392–404). Routledge.

Gregory, A., Valin, J., & Virmani, S. (2023). Humans needed more than ever. An analysis of the use of AI in PR and the impact on public relations work. Chartered Institute of Public Relations. Available at: https://www.cipr.co.uk/CIPR/Our_work/Policy/AI_in_PR_/AI_in_PR_guides.aspx?WebsiteKey=0379ffac-bc76-433c-9a94-56a04331bf64

Halford, S. (2018). *Gender, power and organisations: An introduction*. Bloomsbury Publishing.

Halrynjo, S., & Lyng, S. T. (2009). Preferences, constraints or schemas of devotion? Exploring Norwegian mothers' withdrawals from high-commitment Careers 1. *The British Journal of Sociology, 60*(2), 321–343. 10.1111/j.1468-4446.2009.01233.x

Hammer, R. (2023). Between Stuart Hall and Cedric Robinson: Capturing imaginaries of racial capitalism. Sociology of Race and Ethnicity, Volume 9, Issue 2

Hassan, R. (2018). It's high time PR learned to 'speak Muslim'. *PR Week*. Retrieved from: https://www.prweek.com/article/1485370/its-high-time-pr-learned-speak-muslim?utm_source=dlvr.it&utm_medium=facebook

Haynes, B, (2011). The impact of generational differences on the workplace. Journal of Corporate Real Estate, 13 (2), 98–108

Hesmondhalgh, D., & Baker, S. (2013). *Creative labour: Media work in three cultural industries*. Routledge.

Hideg, I., Shen, W., & Koval, C. Z. (2024). Hear, hear! A review of accent discrimination at work. *Current Opinion in Psychology, 60,* 101906. https://doi.org/10.1016/j.copsyc.2024.101906

Jackson, S. E., & Joshi, A. (2004). Diversity in social context: A multi-attribute, multilevel analysis of team diversity and sales performance. *Journal of Organizational Behavior, 25*(6), 675–702. https://doi.org/10.1002/job.265

Jensen, R. (2021) *Whiteness*. In Caliendo, S. M., & McIlwain, C. D. (Eds.). (2021). *The Routledge companion to race and ethnicity*. London: Routledge.

Jones, G. B., Chace, B. C., & Wright, J. M. (2020). Cultural diversity drives innovation: Empowering teams for success. *International Journal of Innovation Science, 12*(3), 323–343. https://doi.org/10.1108/ijis-04-2020-0042

Kim, B. (2021). How promoting disability inclusion establishes a strong workplace. *PR Week*. Retrieved from: https://www.prweek.com/article/1730320/promoting-disability-inclusion-establishes-strong-workplace

Kim, R., Roberson, L., Russo, M., & Briganti, P. (2019). Language diversity, nonnative accents, and their consequences at the workplace: Recommendations for individuals, teams, and organizations. *The Journal of Applied Behavioral Science*, *55*(1), 73–95. https://doi.org/10.1177/0021886318800997

Konrad, A. M., Ross, G., & Linnehan, F. (2006). Is promoting an African American Unfair? The triple interaction of participant ethnicity, target ethnicity, and ethnic identity 1. *Journal of Applied Social Psychology*, *36*(5), 1215–1233. https://doi.org/10.1111/j.0021-9029.2006.00039.x

Korn, Ferry. (nd). *Will AI help or hurt diversity and inclusion?* Retrieved from: https://www.kornferry.com/insights/featured-topics/diversity-equity-inclusion/will-ai-help-or-hurt-diversity-and-inclusion

Kossek, E. E., Lobel, S. A., & Brown, A. J. (2005). Human resource strategies to manage workforce diversity. In A. M. Konrad, P. Prasad, & J. M. Pringle (Eds.), *Handbook of workplace diversity* (pp. 54–74). Sage.

Lenney, E. (1977). Women's self-confidence in achievement settings. *Psychological Bulletin, 84*(1), 1–13. https://doi.org/10.1037/0033-2909.84.1.1

Litzler, E., Samuelson, C. C., & Lorah, J. A. (2014). Breaking it down: Engineering student STEM confidence at the intersection of race/ethnicity and gender. *Research in Higher Education*, *55*, 810–832. https://doi.org/10.1007/s11162-014-9333-z

Logan, N. (2011). The White leader prototype: A critical analysis of race in public relations. *Journal of Public Relations Research, 23*(4), 442–457. https://doi.org/10.1080/1062726X.2011.605974

Logan, N. (2023). Public relations and the racial reckoning. Exploring race, activism, and black matter lives. In D. Pompper, K. R. Place, and C. K. Weaver (Eds.), *The Routledge companion of public relations* (Chapter 3, pp. 46–60). Rouldedge.

Marschlich, S., & Ingenhoff, D. (2021). The role of public relations in corporate diplomacy: how relationship cultivation increases organizational legitimacy. *Journal of Public Relations Research, 33*(2), 86–105. https://doi.org/10.1080/1062726X.2021.1981332

Mayorga-Gallo, S. (2019). The White-centering logic of diversity ideology. *American Behavioral Scientist, 63*(13), 1789–1809. https://doi.org/10.1177/0002764219842619

Men, L. R., Qin, Y. S., Mitson, R., & Thelen, P. (2023). Engaging employees via an inclusive climate: the role of organizational diversity communication and cultural intelligence. Journal of Public Relations Research, 35(5–6), 450–471

Moore-Berg, S. L., & Karpinski, A. (2021). Race and social class as intersecting social categories: An analysis of implicit and explicit attitudes. *Social Psychology (Göttingen, Germany)*, *52*(4), 227–237. https://doi.org/10.1027/1864-9335/a000451

Mor Barak, M. E. (2000). The inclusive workplace: An ecosystems approach to diversity management. *Social Work*, *45*(4), 339–353.

Mottaz, C. J. (1987). Age and work satisfaction. *Work and Occupations*, *14*(3), 387–409. https://doi.org/10.1177/0730888487014003004

Müller, W., & Pollak, R. (2015). Mobility, social. In J. D. Wright (Ed.), *International encyclopedia of the social & behavioral Sciences* (2nd ed., pp. 640–646). Elsevier.

Mundy, D. (2015). From principle to policy to practice? Diversity as a driver of multicultural, stakeholder engagement in public relations. Public Relations Journal, 9(1), 1–20.

Munshi, D., & Kurian, P. (2022). The public strikes back: Subaltern organizing and insurgent public relations. In *The Routledge companion to public relations* (pp. 405–415). Routledge.

NHS Communicate. (2024). *The state of NHS communications*. Retrieved from: https://nhsproviders.org/media/698260/state-of-comms-profession-24-report.pdf

Ortí, A. (2010). La apertura y el enfoque cualitativo o estructural: la entrevista abierta semidirectiva y la discusión de grupo. In M. García-Ferrando, J. Ibáñez and F. Alvira (Eds.), *El análisis de la realidad social. Métodos y técnicas de investigación* (pp. 219–282). Alianza Editorial.

Pompper, D. (2005). "Difference" in public relations research: A case for introducing critical race theory. *Journal of Public Relations Research, 17*(2), 139–169. https://doi.org/10.1207/s1532754xjprr1702_5

Pompper, D. (2007). The gender-ethnicity construct in public relations organizations: Using feminist standpoint theory to discover Latinas' realities. *The Howard Journal of Communications, 18*(4), 291–311. https://doi.org/10.1080/1064617070 1653669

Pompper, D. (2013). *Diversity in the Public Relations Industry: How practitioners are pushing back to make change.* Routledge.

PR Academy Ltd. (2024, February 9). This week there have been conversations around apprenticeships and AI, freelancing, diversity, equity and inclusion (DEI), and what follows social media. *LinkedIn.* Retrieved from: https://www.linkedin.com/posts/pr-academy-ltd_this-week-in-pr-9-february-newsletter-activity-7161639 702708633601-Zna4/

PRCA Race and Ethnicity Equity Board. (2024). *From words to change. Four years on: Ethnicity pay gap reporting in the communications sector.* Retrieved from: https://www.flipsnack.com/prcauk/from-words-to-change/full-view.html

Randle, K., Forson, C., & Calveley, M. (2015). Towards a Bourdieusian analysis of the social composition of the UK film and television workforce. *Work, Employment and Society, 29*(4), 590–606. https://doi.org/10.1177/0950017014542498

Rawat, S. (2023). Disability and neurodiversity in PR – How to make your business more accessible. *PR Week.* Retrieved from: https://www.prweek.co.uk/article/1828221/disability-neurodiversity-pr-%E2%80%93-business-accessible

Sha, B. L., & Ford, R. (2007). Redefining "requisite variety": The challenge of multiple diversities for the future of public relations excellence. In E. L. Toth (Ed.), *The future of excellence in public relations and communication management: Challenges for the next generation* (pp. 381–398). Lawrence Erlbaum Associates Publishers.

Shen, J., Chanda, A., D'Netto, B., & Monga, M. (2009). Managing diversity through human resource management: An international perspective and conceptual framework. *The International Journal of Human Resource Management, 20*(2), 235–251. https://doi.org/10.1080/09585190802670516

Shen, H., & Jiang, H. (2013). Profiling public relations practitioners' work-life conflict: From a diversity lens. *Public Relations Journal, 7*(2), 71–95.

Smith, R. D. (2020). *Strategic planning for public relations.* Routledge.

Smudde, P. M. (2021). Internal public relations' role with workplace, spirituality, and religion. *Public Relations Review, 47*(5), 102121. https://doi.org/10.1016/j.pubrev.2021.102121

Social Mobility Commission. (2022). *State of the Nation 2022: A fresh approach to social mobility.* Retrieved from: https://assets.publishing.service.gov.uk/media/62b2e45b8fa8f5357a677f29/State_of_the_Nation_2022_A_fresh_approach_to_social_mobility.pdf

Socially Mobile. (n.d.). *About socially mobile.* Retrieved from: https://www.socially-mobile.org.uk/about

Sison, M. D. (2016). Diversity and inclusion in Australian public relations: Towards a multiple perspectives approach. *Media International Australia, 160*(1), 32–42. https://doi.org/10.1177/1329878X16651140

Taylor Bennett Foundation. (n.d.). *PR training programme.* Retrieved from: https://www.taylorbennettfoundation.org/pr-training-programme-candidates/

Tilson, D. J., & Venkateswaran, A. (2006). Toward a covenantal model of public relations: Hindu faith communities and devotional–promotional communication. *Journal of Media and Religion, 5*(2), 111–133. https://doi.org/10.1207/s15328415 jmr0502_3

Tindall, N. T. J., & Waters, R. D. (2012). Coming out to tell our stories: Using queer theory to understand the career experiences of gay men in public relations, *Journal of Public Relations Research, 24*(5), 451–475. https://doi.org/10.1080/1062726X.2012.723279

Townsend, S. (2003). Book Review: Muhr, T. 1997. ATLAS.ti 5: The Knowledge Workbench. Berlin: Scientific Software Development. For PC and Mac. *Papers from the Institute of Archaeology*, *14*, 161–169. https://doi.org/10.5334/pia.191

Trevisan, F. (2017). Crowd-sourced advocacy: Promoting disability rights through online storytelling. *Public Relations Inquiry*, *6*(2), 191–208. https://doi.org/10.1177/2046147X17697785

Tsetsura, K. (2012). A struggle for legitimacy: Russian women secure their professional identities in public relations in a hyper-sexualized patriarchal workplace. *Public Relations Journal*, *6*(1), 1–21.Vardeman-Winter, J., Tindall, N., & Jiang, J. (2013). Intersectionality and publics: How exploring publics' multiple identities questions basic public relations concepts. *Public Relations Inquiry, 2*(3), 279–304. https://doi.org/10.1177/2046147X13491564

Vardeman-Winter, J., & Place, K. (2017). Still a lily-white field of women: The state of workforce diversity in public relations practice and research. *Public Relations Review, 2*(43), 326–336. https://doi.org/10.1016/j.pubrev.2017.01.004

Vardeman, J., & Sebesta, A. (2020). The problem of intersectionality as an approach to digital activism: The women's march on Washington's attempt to unite all women. *Journal of Public Relations Research, 32*, 7–29. https://doi.org/10.1080/1062726X.2020.1716769

Vasco, A. (2024, November 04). Representation alone isn't enough. *LinkedIn*. Retrieved from: https://www.linkedin.com/posts/adam-vasco-90429814a_representation-alone-isnt-enough-in-the-activity-7258766787675140096-Hm7E?utm_source=share&utm_medium=member_desktop

Waddington, S. (2024). *LinkedIn post*. Retrieved from: https://www.linkedin.com/posts/stephenwaddington_fundraising-for-socially-mobile-this-year-activity-7264021083597553666-4moL?utm_source=share&utm_medium=member_desktop

Warde, A. (2019). Extending the sociology of consumption. Rassegna Italiana di Sociologia, 60(3), 616–626.

Waymer, D., & Heath, R. L. (2016). Critical race and public relations: The case of environmental racism and risk bearer agency. In J. L'Etang, D. McKie, & N. Snow (Eds.), *The Routledge handbook of critical public relations* (pp. 313–326). Routledge.

Weiss, M., Weiss, D., & Zacher, H. (2022). All set in stone? How essentialist beliefs about aging affect older workers' motivation to continue working beyond retirement age. *Journal of Organizational Behavior*, *43*(8), 1446–1461. https://doi.org/10.1002/job.2647

UK Black Comms Network. (2024). *One step forward, two steps black.* Retrieved from: https://static1.squarespace.com/static/5eeb1c625cddf3179c2d330d/t/66ad2c2ad913620d936ac4a1/1722625081718/BCN_Report_2024_FINAL.pdf

White, R., Bornman, J., Johnson, E., & Msipa, D. (2021). Court accommodations for persons with severe communication disabilities: A legal scoping review. *Psychology, Public Policy, and Law*, *27*(3), 399. https://doi.org/10.1037/law0000289

White-Sax, B. (2024). Disability and neurodiversity in PR – how to make your business more accessible. *PR Week*. Retrieved from: https://www.prweek.com/article/1828221/disability-neurodiversity-pr-%E2%80%93-business-accessible

Wigley, S., & Zhang, W. (2014). Does planning and practice make perfect? A study of communication culture, autonomy and PR practitioners' confidence in handling crises. *Public Relations Journal*, *8*(2), 1–13

Williams, J. (2023). Putting the D into ESG - making PR workplaces accessible for disabled staff. *PR Week.* Retrieved from: https://www.prweek.com/article/1813783/putting-d-esg-%E2%80%93-making-pr-workplaces-accessible-disabled-staff

Xifra, J. (2008). Soccer, civil religion, and public relations: Devotional–promotional communication and Barcelona Football Club. *Public Relations Review*, 34(2) pp. 192–198.

Index

Note: **Bold** page numbers refer to tables.

For Product Safety Concerns and Information please contact our EU representative GPSR@taylorandfrancis.com Taylor & Francis Verlag GmbH, Kaufingerstraße 24, 80331 München, Germany

Printed and bound by CPI Group (UK) Ltd, Croydon, CR0 4YY
14/09/2026
02216243-0002